NEAR

DEATH-EXPERIENCES

AFTERLIFE

FROM ISLAMIC PERSPECTIVE

COMPILE BY

MUHAMMAD MOHEE

UDDIN IBN AHMAD

Near
Death-Experiences

Afterlife from Islamic perspective

Muhammad Mohee Uddin

First paperback edition November 2021
ISBN: 9781666250954

For information about special discounts available for bulk purchases, sales promotions, fund-raising and educational needs, contact: mohee1990@outlook.com

TABLE OF CONTENTS

1. OUT OF BODY EXPERIENCES (OBE)

In 2011, Mr A, a 57-year-old social worker from England, was admitted to Southampton General Hospital after collapsing at work. Medical personnel were in the middle of inserting a catheter into his groin when he went into cardiac arrest. With oxygen cut off, his brain immediately flat-lined. Mr A died.

Despite this, he remembers what happened next. The staff grabbed an automated external defibrillator (AED), a shock-delivery machine used to try to reactivate the heart. Mr A heard a mechanical voice twice say, "Shock the patient." In between those orders, he looked up to see a strange woman beckoning to him from the back corner of the room, near the ceiling. He joined her, leaving his inert body behind. "I felt that she knew me, I felt that I could trust her, and I felt she was there for a reason [but] I didn't know what that was," Mr A later recalled. "The next second, I was up there, looking down at me, the nurse and another man who had a bald head."

Hospital records later verified the AED's two verbal commands. Mr A's descriptions of the people in the room – people he had not seen before he lost consciousness – and their actions were also accurate. He was describing things that happened during a three-minute window of time that, according to what we know about biology, he should not have had any awareness of.

Near death experiences ranged from terrifying to blissful. There were those who reported feeling afraid or suffering persecution, for example. "I had to get through a ceremony … and the ceremony was to get burned," one patient recalled. "There were four men with me, and whichever lied would die … I saw men in coffins being buried upright." Another remembered being "dragged through deep water", and still another was "told I was going to die and the quickest way was to say the last short word I could remember".

Others, however, experienced the opposite sensation, with 22% reporting "a feeling of peace or pleasantness". Some saw living things: "All plants, no flowers" or "lions and tigers"; while others basked in the glow of "a brilliant light" or were reunited with family. Some, meanwhile, reported a strong sense of deja-vu: "I felt like I knew what people were going to do before they did it". Heightened senses, a distorted perception of the passage of time and a feeling of disconnection from the body were also common sensations that survivors reported.

2. MAN BELIEVES HE SAW ANGELS

After his colon burst, a man named Jamie suffered life-threatening injuries. While surgeons were attempting to save Jamie's life, he believes he saw the afterlife.

He said that he was greeted by angels in a heavenly realm who gave him guidance on his life.

Jamie wrote on the Near Death Experience Research Foundation: "I was in a beautiful space that was filled with light.

"A male angel, whom I cannot describe other than as a being of light, was talking calmly to me.

"He told me that everything was going to be all right.

"I was going to come through this emergency and go on to live a very long and pleasant life.

"He said I would have little things happen as they do in life, but nothing really bad would happen to me.

"I would have mostly peace and much joy in my life. It was the most peaceful experience I have ever had.

"I was told that I had nothing to be afraid of and everything to live for."

3. Matthew Botsford

Matthew Botsford was standing outside an Atlanta restaurant when a shot rang out. Two men who'd been denied entry into the establishment moments earlier, in what has to be one of the most over-the-top customer service freakouts of all time, were indiscriminately firing at the front of the building. One of the bullets hit Botsford in the head. He remembers feeling a pain like a hot needle driving into his skull, then falling to the pavement, at which point everything went black. He died three times on the way to and at the hospital before doctors finally put him into a medically-induced coma that lasted for 27 days.

His descriptions of the things he saw while in that coma are nothing short of terrifying. Things began with him shackled at his wrists and ankles, suspended in midair over a deep, glowing red pit. Inside the pit, four-legged creatures roamed the floor while smoke billowed up from the magma below. Each plume of smoke contained exactly one tortured soul, suffering all alone.

That's something else Botsford made note of ... the isolation. All around him he could hear the screams of millions of damned souls, but their company was meaningless, because he understood that he was by himself and that this would last for eternity.

He's kind of overstating that loneliness, though, because at one point, a team of demons showed up to eat his flesh right from the bone, only to have it immediately grow back so they could eat it again.

Finally, he was spared when a gigantic hand reached through the wall and pulled him out. As it did, he heard someone say, "It's not your time.

4. Man believes he brought 'shadowy' figures back from afterlife

Following an unknown injury, a person named Roman was rushed to hospital. Doctors were unable to figure out his condition as Roman slipped in and out of consciousness for over a week. Each time, Roman believes he saw the afterlife where he was greeted by a mysterious figure in a sea of light.

However, since his recovery, Roman now believes he sees these figures in the real world.

Roman wrote on the Near Death Experience Research Foundation: "I found myself walking down a hallway with a male figure who was much taller than my 6'2" self.

"I never saw the man's face, but I remember him asking me, 'Are you ready? Are you on board?'

"I always answered the same way, 'Yes, I'm ready. I'm on board.' As we walked side-by-side toward a bright light at the end of the hallway, there were many people walking the other way.

"None of these people made eye contact or spoke, but they seemed to be walking in a very determined manner away from the light.

"I never got to the end of the hallway, so I don't know what was beyond the light. This went on for over eight days of a 10-day stay in the hospital.

"Since that time, I am constantly seeing small shadowy figures in my peripheral vision that seem to vanish when I turn my head."

5. WOMAN BELIEVES SHE WAS TURNED AWAY FROM HEAVEN

A person named Susannah temporarily died after falling and hitting her head. Before she was resuscitated by paramedics, Susannah believes she gained the answer to the age old question: What happens when you die?

Susannah believes she was offered a glimpse of the afterlife, where she was showered in love by a human-like figure.

The being was supposedly made entirely of light, who controlled whether she entered the afterlife or not.

Susannah wrote on the Near Death Experience Research Foundation: "He was very bright and seemed human but was not, he was so bright that he was quite hard to see or recognise.

"He was pleased to see me but did not seem to think I should be there.

"He said that he would go and ask what to do - if I should be there. The words were just 'felt' not spoken.

"I waited outside the entrance sort of floating in the love. It was so beautiful and so perfect.

"I had never felt anything even close to this and was just in absolute 'heaven' and did not want it to ever end.

"I felt completely loved and that nothing bad could ever happen. This seemed to last for a long time.

"Then the light person/being returned and said that he was sorry but it was not my time, it was the wrong time.

"I was absolutely devastated. I went quickly back to my body and my thoughts were, 'Oh no, back to this horrible world.'"

6. MAN BELIEVES HE CROSSED INTO 'PERFECT' REALM

Following an accident as a child, a man named Chris believes he was taken to the afterlife. While Chris was not clinically dead, he was unconscious for several minutes following an accident, and believes he saw the afterlife. The afterlife, according to Chris, consists of being bathed in a "formless" light where one instantly forgets about what came before.

He also said that the place he was in was "perfect" where he was no longer a physical being.

Writing on the Near Death Experience Research Foundation, Chris said: "I suddenly found myself in a different realm. It was formless, light, and colourful. I didn't see anyone. It was like a soft, light-bath.

"I was fully surrounded in and a part of this light. I felt at one with the light and at peace. I was definitely 'me,' but I didn't' have a body. In this place, my old life didn't exist.

"I had no thought of the life on earth. I was just there, and 'there' was perfect.

"Then I felt a strange, sucking sensation. It felt like I was being pulled into and becoming something else at the same time.

"As I got closer, I could see my old life coming back to me. I suddenly remembered I had this other life with school, family, and friends.

"I had a sinking feeling of 'oh no, not this' and I knew I'd have to face all the mess of normal life again.

"I even had this feeling about my own family. Although I loved them, my family was imperfect and unhappy in many ways.

"The realm I visited is so hard to quantify or describe, because it was totally formless so it was purely a subjective experience. There is no way to explain it to other people

"When I came back to my body, I recognised my life with the feeling of 'oh this thing again.' It was as if I had forgotten about this life, but then remembered it only when I came back into the body."

7. WOMAN BELIEVES SHE SAW HELL

Following an accidental overdose, a woman named Stephanie temporarily died. While most people claim to see a light at the end of a tunnel or a heavenly realm, Stephanie believes she saw Hell. In her experience, Stephanie said that she could sense she was somewhere evil and could see carnage all around her.

However, since her near death experience, Stephanie believes she was given an opportunity to turn her life around or else face the prospect of spending "eternity suffering in Hell".

She wrote on the Near Death Experience Research Foundation: "I fell backwards and continued falling for what seemed like forever.

"I saw glimpses of my life from the very beginning and only visions of everything I had ever done wrong.

"I kept falling until I found myself in the middle of the city where I was born. It looked like the city had been hit by a bomb and I was the only person there.

"I had an overwhelming feeling that I was in Hell. I had been shown the reasons why God sent me to Hell while I was falling. I knew that I had caused myself this outcome and I knew it was too late to change.

"Then suddenly I was back in my body and I was alive! I was so excited and grateful for God blessing me with this wake up call.

"I have gone from questioning if God existed; to sharing this story with others in hope of it changing other people's lives.

"I was shown that if I didn't get my life together now, I would spend eternity suffering in Hell. Heaven has to exist because I know for sure that I've been to Hell.

"I know I never want to spend eternity living alone with nothing but my mistakes and guilt holding me down."

8. MAN BELIEVES HE WAS GREETED INTO BLACKNESS BY MYSTERIOUS FIGURES

A person named Steve was working a security guard in New Orleans, US, when he was confronted by armed robbers. After an altercation, Steve said that he was shot by his assailants who left him to die.

Thankfully, Steve was discovered and saved by paramedics, but for a brief few minutes, he was clinically dead.

It was his time when he was clinically dead where Steve believes he caught a glimpse of the afterlife.

In it, Steve believes he was entombed in a black void but was eventually shown the way out by mysterious figures.

Steve wrote on the Near Death Experience Research Foundation: "The next thing I knew, I was in a sort of 'black box,' like a very dark void. It was neither pleasant nor unpleasant.

"I was aware of 'myself', Steve, but I didn't seem to have a physical body.

"I was wondering where I was with all this blackness surrounding me—but I was definitely aware of myself.

"Next appeared a vertical line of bright, white light, from the highest to the lowest point in front of me.

"The light started to open, as a door would. Two heads stuck out through the emergent opening and were peering at me.

"They were not too close, but not too far away. I struggled to focus on them.

"One of the Beings appeared to be wearing a white hat and the other Being, a black hat.

"Both Beings had large black eyes. Finally, both Beings slowly withdrew the way they had entered, through the contracting 'doorway' of light, which then closed completely. The bright light dissipated. Only darkness remained."

Suddenly, Steve was back in his body but he is now convinced there is an afterlife.

9. WOMAN RECOUNTS BRUSH WITH DEATH AS A CHILD

A woman known only as Barbara S to protect her privacy has revealed what she thinks happened after she almost died as a child. Although the event occurred more than 50 years ago, when aged 10, the woman recounted her story to the Near-Death Experience Foundation (NDERF) in remarkable detail.

She said: "It was a beautiful sunny summer day when I was at our family's wood cabin in northern Michigan.

"In front of the cabin was a river. The water was perfectly clear. I could not swim at the time.

"I was wading out in the water and the water was at chest height. I was looking at the sky and listening to nature and I took another step out and found there was no bottom and I went under the water and the river started to move me to the right.

"The last thing I remember thinking and seeing in my body, was that I could see so far underwater and that the water was so clear."

It was then Barbara believes she had a supernatural experience.

She said: "The next thing I remember was I came into this clear white light.

"As soon as I came into this light, all my fear of drowning was gone and I felt this light envelop me.

"This clear white light was all around me that I could see.

"I didn't look behind me but I know it was behind me too. I felt this total love and acceptance of me and I felt the same with the light.

"I knew I was part of this light; I belonged to this light. I was home.

"I then realised there was a presence in this light and I realised I was light, too."

The woman then attempts to articulate the episode's almost incomprehensible nature.

She said: "We were the same but with different personalities. I couldn't see anybody for myself or a body in the light.

"The light then told me 'you are here to learn how to love and to gain knowledge'.

"When I was told this, all the implications of the word love and knowledge were imparted to me.

With the word 'love', it wasn't just about physical love but the love of nature, accepting all people as the same, everything that pertained to love.

"The same was with knowledge. It wasn't just about book knowledge but about learning about different cultures, histories of the world.

"I felt when I was told this that it wasn't just my reason for being on Earth but all of our reason for being here: mankind."

She added how she believes the event had a profound impact on her life.

Barbara said: " When I look back over my life I can see I have been doing exactly what I was told to do in the light that day.

"My life has been all about learning and since I have been on the net, I have made many friends all over the world.

"There was no time there. I don't know if I was only there for seconds, minutes or what.

"I knew my body was safe when I came into the light. I knew I was going back to my body.

"I don't remember leaving the light. I don't remember getting back into my body. That has all been blocked."

Stories involving people reportedly experiencing such events have been recounted by those brought back from the brink of death since the time of Greek philosopher such as Sophocles.

10. 'THERE WAS NOTHING BUT AN OVERWHELMING PRESENCE'

A person named Jim, who was previously diagnosed with diabetes, temporarily died following an episode which left him unconscious. Jim has detailed his experience in extraordinary detail, which may provide an insight into what happens when we die.

Jim said that as he slipped into what he perceived to be the afterlife, he experienced nothing.

Jim said that everything faded to black, and he was blessed with an unshakeable sense of peace.

However, Jim said that there was an overwhelming presence which spoke to him telepathically.

Jim wrote on the Near Death Experience Research Foundation: "I felt an indescribable peace and calm. It's hard to put into words but I have never felt such a feeling before in my life.

"To simply say that I felt calm and peaceful does not do it justice. Low blood sugar, once consciousness returns, produces intense feelings of anxiety, agitation, confusion, fear and panic.

"I felt none of this. Quite the opposite. I have never felt such peace, calm, warmth and love in my life.

"There were no tunnels, bright lights or life reviews.

"What I did experience was a presence, which reassured me that everything would be all right.

"It was not a spoken voice but rather a telepathic message, which was just as clear as a spoken voice. It reassured me and put me at ease.

Suddenly Jim was back in his body.

11. TIME LOSES ALL MEANING IN THE AFTERLIFE

Time is very much a human concept, based on the idea of entropy - randomised chaos within the Universe which gives the illusion of passing time. However, away from our Earthly realm, one person believes time loses its significance in the afterlife.

A man who just gave his name as Bob temporarily died following an accidental fall from a three story building.

Before he could be revived, Bob believes he saw the afterlife, where he was greeted by all of his dead relatives.

Time in that world lost all meaning, with everything happening all at once, according to Bob.

He wrote on the Near Death Experience Research Foundation: "The light was strong and somewhat unearthly at the end of a long tunnel. The light was as much love as anything in that it was pervasive.

"My relatives (all deceased) were there, all at their prime in life. They were dressed (I would say 1940's style which would have been prime years for most).

"Relatives I knew of, such as my grandfathers, but never knew in life were there as well as uncles and aunts who passed before I knew them.

"The unconditional love was overwhelming and permeated all of us genuinely and richly.

"There was no element of time and no verbally spoken word. Both time and verbal communication are of this world not needed in the NDE world.

"Everything was open thought communication. Time is the invention of man in this world, not a part of our core spirit.

"All of this was very clear to me in the NDE. Any question or uncertainty was confirmed, known, through non-verbal understanding."

12. WOMAN MEETS HIGHER POWER IN AFTERLIFE WHO CHANGED HER FOR LIFE

A person named Gabby was clinically dead - which is the cessation of the heart beat or breath - for a short amount of time following an accidental overdose on medicine. Before she could be revived, Gabby believes she spent time in the afterlife.

While there, she believes she met an unspecified higher being, who told her to turn around and go back to her normal body.

However, the experience has completely changed her outlook on life.

Gabby wrote on the Near Death Experience Research Foundation: "I watched the doctor say 'we are losing her, we are losing her.'

"Then, I was in a tunnel and travelling to a light with a wonderful feeling of love and protection.

"A voice said 'why have you stopped fighting? Don't you know I am still with you?' I was then told that I had to go back.

"I did not want to, but I woke up in a body that had voided and was really manly.

"The doctor was almost in tears and said 'we nearly lost you'

13. AFTERLIFE CONSISTS OF FLYING THROUGH THE UNIVERSE

A person known as Lee was temporarily but clinically dead - which is the cessation of the heart or breathing - and believes he saw a glimpse of the afterlife. Instead of rolling meadows or fluffy white clouds, Lee claims the afterlife consists of zooming through the Universe.

Lee suffered his near death experience after slipping into a diabetic induced coma, and now believes he has a greater understanding of the cosmos.

Writing on the Near Death Experience Research Foundation, Lee said: "I instantly shot out of my body, but I was not above myself.

"It was as if I was some kind of energy, and I was flying away from earth. Then it seemed as if I was flying away from the solar system.

"Then I started flying away faster and I saw bunches of stars as if they were galaxies flying away from me.

"Then they seemed to be bunching together into huge packs as if they were separate universes or something like that.

"It was as if there was a force or energy out there way bigger than anything we know, and I had an enormous sense of understanding the meaning of life, that's when I seemed to shoot back at a phenomenal speed!

"As it was happening, I remember feeling very excited and thinking to myself 'So that's why we are here!'.

"And it was so real, but my understanding was not explained to me.

"Due to this experience, my view on life after death goes somewhere way beyond planet earth and our energy possibly passes to another dimension or a different universe."

14. 'BEINGS MADE OF LIGHT BROUGHT ME BACK TO LIFE'

A person named Ione was clinically, albeit briefly, dead following complications during abdominal surgery. While her death was brief before she was resuscitated, Ione believes she saw the afterlife in an experience which lasted a perceived eternity.

While she was there, Ione believes she saw beings made of light which brought her back to the earthly realm.

Writing on the Near Death Experience Research Foundation, Ione said: "I found myself in a dark place with four Beings around a table. They wore hooded cloaks.

"The light shone out of the front of the hoods, like a glowing light. Their hands were also made of light.

"I was located at my head but just slightly under the table and out of the way.

"These Beings worked very swiftly but they were certain in what each one of them had to do.

"There was no talking between them but it was a very coordinated effort.

"They may have been communicating telepathically but I'm not sure.

"I heard a humming type of noise, but I think it was coming from the other world. I couldn't understand any words.

"When the Beings were finished with my adjustments, I found myself instantly back in the earthly world and heading toward my physical body."

15. WOMAN RECOUNTS 'TRAVELLING THROUGH TUNNEL'

A female identified only as C.D has described the incredible experience she believes happened to her on the operating table more than 40 years ago. C.D told of her time what she thinks occurred following issues with a surgical to the Near Death Experience Research Foundation (NDERF) blog.

In 1978, while undergoing surgery for a blood clot in her head, the woman experienced something numerous others have in similar situations.

She said: "I went out of my body. Saw the doctors around working on me during surgery.

"I went through a tunnel really fast. I was in a wonderful light. I saw a bridge.

Across the bridge were people I knew who had died, like my father who had died less than a year before this.

"He was so happy to see me and said, 'Hi Mija'.

"There was light around them. Other family members were all smiling at me.

"He was so proud for them to see me. I was happy to be there."

However, it was then that she learned her time in what she feels was the afterlife came to an abrupt end.

She said: "Then after a while, a voice said I had to go back. It wasn't my time.

"I had things to do. My dad's face dropped. He looked sad.

"I said I didn't want to go back. I was crying.

"Then like an instant. I went back through the tunnel and I was back in my body."

16. WOMAN RECOUNTS 'ASCENDING AT PEACE' AFTER NEAR

The woman, known only as Mache G to protect her privacy, has narrated an extraordinary episode which bears many of the hallmarks of an epiphany. In 1980, when Mache was a mere four or five years old, she was struck by a fever which only got worse as the days passed.

She told the Near-Death Experience Foundation site: "Mom took me to the hospital when she realised that I was getting worse.

"I was immediately rushed back to the emergency room beds.

"I just wanted to sleep for a while. I remember telling everyone I was feeling much better.

"The sounds in the room started to get a hollow echo to them. I wanted to close my eyes, so I did."

And it was then her incredible story of what she believes happened begins.

She said: "I wasn't upset or scared. But, I was a little confused.

"I knew I didn't have a body. I felt like I was part of everything and everyone.

"I just floated up and could see other rooms. I later detailed conversations that there is no way I could have known.

"I lifted out of the hospital and continued ascending.

"I began browsing through time. I saw events from my short life.

"I later detailed things that occurred before I could even talk.

"These were events I should not be able to remember but I do and in great detail.

"As I kept ascending, I felt at peace. There were no questions or unknowns.

"Time wrapped in on itself. There was no past, present, or future as we see it here.

"Everything happened now and all at one time. I felt no fears or worries.

"I began drifting towards a beautiful light and I wanted to touch it."

However, it was then when her experience come to an abrupt end.

She said: "Suddenly there was a pop. It felt like I was attached to a cord when someone grabbed it and jerked me down. I descended almost instantly."

17. She felt 'like energy' as she entered bright light

The woman, who only introduced herself as Beth, shared the incredible details of her near-death experience (NDE). Beth was undergoing a c-section for her third child when she started bleeding out on the operating table. When the doctors could not stop the haemorrhage, Beth recalls seeing her blood pressure drop until her heart stopped.

Then, she vividly recalls finding herself in a place of bright light.

She said: "I wasn't in human form, rather, I felt like myself but as energy.

"I spoke but not with words. I spoke with mental energy or something along those lines.

"Other people or energies were there. There were people I knew who were there.

"I could feel love and a peaceful, contented feeling."

And although Beth could not recognise any of the other people, she felt as though she knew them.

She claims they reached out to her telepathically in the same way she communicated with them.

Beth said: "I remember sensing them and hearing sounds that were reminders of things I've been through in my waking life.

"I was told so many things, although some are hard to remember now."

As this went on, Beth was told this was not her time to die because she had not "completed life".

She then described an odd sensation, like a telephone ringing.

Beth then woke up to see her eldest daughter standing over her.

She said: "I told her that I was sorry that I'd been gone for hours. She told mom that it had only been around a minute that I had been gone.

"I felt as though I was away for six or more hours. I retained so many positive feelings and knowledge in less than a minute.

"I don't know what the right words to describe the things that were spoken to me through the energy."

18. WOMAN BELIEVES 'SILHOUETTED FIGURES GAVE HER ALL EARTHLY KNOWLEDGE'

A person who gives her name as just Shirley temporarily died following complications during surgery. Thankfully, Shirley was brought back from the dead but believes she saw the afterlife in her brush with death. Shirley described how she perceived the afterlife to be something completely different to what we are used to on Earth.

She believes silhouetted figures parade in an otherworldly light where she was given all the knowledge in the world in an instant.

Shirley detailed her perceived moment in the afterlife on the Near Death Experience Research Foundation.

She said: "I was a silhouette of dark grey with light grey surrounding the whole area, except for the bright light that seemed to be heading up.

"The light being was not of Earth light. There was no need for the Moon or stars.

"The best way I can describe the light is it was like the look of a full Moon brightness.

"Other silhouettes were moving through the tunnel of light at an upward angle. Each silhouette was alone.

"I couldn't tell the gender of man or woman or child. There were no animals. There was no colour in what I saw. The feeling of happiness and complete understanding of everything of Earth was known in a flash.

"I was home, really home. Nothing of earth was present. The only thing there was me and information entering my mind.

19. MAN CLAIMS HE MET SATAN IN HELL

Van who claims to have had a life-changing experience after temporarily dying 26 years ago. According to Van's testimony, he collapsed dead for about 30 minutes after a drugs overdose in 1994.

And though he claims to have died, he has vivid memories of what happened next.

Van said: "Immediately I fell through the earth as if the earth were no longer solid and I were sky diving or something.

"I do not really know how to put this experience into words as there is nothing I can draw upon to explain it except to say that I literally fell through the soil, rocks, minerals, water, etc.

"It was not so much a tunnel as just literally passing through the solids, which at this point were anything but solid."

After falling down for a long time, Van eventually landed on the floor of a mysterious hallway.

Confused and panicked, he tried to find his way out of the otherworldly realm, which he later came to realise was hell.

He saw many doors in the hallway, each with a person inside that was tasked with an arduous punishment of some sorts.

In one room, for instance, a woman was scrubbing a dirty toilet for all eternity.

Eventually, Van claims to have come across a man who identified himself as Satan.

He said: "I immediately stood up and said to him I had to leave and that I should not be here.

"Under normal circumstances, I would dismiss such a person as a lunatic, however, given what I had seen thus far and given what I was feeling inside I half-believed this man.

"I ran out of the room and began running down the hallway again... the endless hallway.

"It felt futile but I was scared and continued running. I could hear the man laughing behind me."

Eventually, Van woke up and saw his friends surrounding him.

He was told he was out cold for about 30 minutes and did not breath the whole time.

20. MAN OPENS UP ABOUT GOING TO HELL

The man who said his name is Michael believes his soul went to hell after suffering from pancreatitis and sepsis nine years ago. During the incident, Michael said he was clinically dead as his heart stopped beating and his organs were failing. As drifted away from life, he told the Near-Death Experience Research Foundation (NDERF) he believes he was transported to hell.

Michael said: "I had pancreatitis that went sepsis and shut down my kidneys and liver, and my heart stopped.

"I went into deep fib. My body swelled and my son said that my eye was almost poking out of my head.

"I went, I believe to hell. There were giant red dragons. The landscape was dark and eerie.

"There were people trapped in what looked like circus carts where they transport lions. They were screaming and bleeding."

Michael was then chased by the red dragons he saw when he first entered hell.

A gold dragon and rider then swooped down towards him and took him away.

Michael said: "Then I was in a room, sitting, talking to my dad who had died in August the same year.

"He told me to let go of the past and move on with my life.

"Then I was at an airport in the winter with snow blowing.

"There was a tram with my children inside but it was covered in ice and I could not get in to talk to them.

"A grape drink was flowing in a fountain inside the tram for them to drink."

The bizarre visions then ended and Michael remembers waking up in an intensive care unit.

Michael believes he pulled through his near-fatal illness with prayers from his friends and relatives.

In the aftermath of the incident, Michael said God definitely exists and so does the afterlife.

21. She Cried to God for second chance

I was bitten by Black Widow spider three times on the arm. I was found by my husband not breathing and without a pulse. It must have been only for a brief period.

In a nutshell, I ended up having to lie on the sofa to try to breathe. I ended up first coming OUT of my body! It was scary for me. VERY scary for me. The only reason I know it happened is that, as I was lying on the sofa with my eyes closed, trying to breathe...all of a sudden, I could see my husband standing at the kitchen sink doing dishes and talking to our daughter who was playing in her highchair with some kind of blue toy.

As I opened my eyes, I saw that the foot of the sofa was about 5 feet below me. I was ready to ask my husband to call 911...but decided against it...and then decided to pray. Note: I hadn't "really" prayed in years. We're talking SERIOUS backsliding here. I fell into all kinds of bad things.

Anyway, as I began to pray, I started to spin and spin and spin. THEN, OK, this is going to sound really whacko, but it's the truth -- you know how people talk about going into a white light? Well, I didn't see a "white" light, but there was a wonderful, calming, warm, homey light that was a color I'd NEVER seen before. The only way I can describe it is a violet/white/blue fluorescent type color -- but it was almost like a pool of color or presence (not a tunnel, really) that was radiating so tremendously. I WANTED to take it in...to go to it...but I DIDN'T, because I knew what it meant.

What I know it meant was that, if I went with that light, I'd be taken from this Earth. I cried inside and asked God to please spare me and give me a second chance at life. I knew that my husband and baby daughter could not stand to live without me (my husband tragically lost his father at 14). I knew the choice wasn't my own...which is why I prayed to the Lord to please give me another chance. I promised to go back to Him...to take him back into my heart...to do things right this time.

The point is that experience has changed my life forever. I'm so grateful for it, but I'm sorry and disappointed that it took that -- something so extreme -- to make me wake up. I'm having a very hard time not hating myself for the bad choices I've made in the past.

Note: Before I was presented with the light/presence, I first went through a period of seeing and feeling several strange shadows kind of wrapping themselves around me and over me...suffocating almost. It was very frightening. This is when I began to beg God's forgiveness and mercy -- for I suspected that these "shadow beings" may have meant that I would not be able to go to God -- but that some horrible alternative would take over.

22. SARAH'S NDE

In August of 1989, I was bicycling home from a volunteer position around 10 p.m. As I was coming up on a light, I was hit from behind by a pickup truck traveling at approximately 50 mph. The bike and I were slammed against the truck. As the driver slammed on the brakes, I was catapulted 60 feet through the air to land on the shoulder of the road. My lungs collapsed, most of my internal organs ruptured, and I broke my pelvis and several ribs. I was pretty close to road kill. Fortunately, a police officer was nearby and able to radio for an ambulance quickly. I, as I know myself, have no memory of the preceding events.

This is what I remember: One moment I was riding my bike and the next, I was in a place of complete darkness. I had no sense of direction or perspective, but I did have an awareness of my body, that is, I still had one. Off in the "distance" I began to notice a hum and a pinprick of light. The sound began to grow louder and the light seemed to be coming toward me. As the object drew closer, I noticed that it was a fantastic demonic creature surrounded by flames with huge eyes and teeth danced toward me slavering and growling. There was menace in its gaze as it smashed its teeth and stuck out a long slobbering orange tongue at me. I was riveted to the "spot" in the dark where I stood. There seemed to be nowhere to go to avoid the thing as the creature was advancing at an increasing speed determined to intercept me. I stood my "ground" and closed my eyes expecting to be engulfed in flames or devoured or both. Instead, I had an awareness of the creature slowly passing painlessly through my body and I turned an inward eye to it only to discover that the creature was laughing with glee as it melted through me. It exited with a pop behind me and suddenly I was flying forward very fast through the dark.

As I flew, two more of the demon creatures came toward me displaying different colors but still fearsome. Armed with my knowledge of the first one, I allowed these beings to approach and pass through me. Soon I came to the entrance of a tunnel in the black. The tunnel seemed to be constructed of gray cloudlike material and wound far away and up to the right. Then it branched and I couldn't see where it led. From the branching on the right extended a yellow white light that helped to softly illuminate the tunnel. I glanced down at myself and noticed that my body was gone. It had been replaced by a blue white light sort of equi-limbed cross/star that pulsed. This "seemed" natural and pleasant to me at the time. It was very freeing to no longer be attached to a weighty form.

Looking back into the tunnel, I noticed there were doorways in both sides of the structure. A few other cross/stars were wandering about in the tunnel, some blue like myself, some amber colored. Two other blue cross/stars appeared beside me and gently propelled me into the tunnel. I floated along and up observing that some "doorways" were open while others seemed to have been shut. The first doorway I peered into resembled a classic Hell. There was the sound of shrieking and agonizing screams. Naked human beings were strewn about a blasted landscape with pools of bubbling excrement and jagged boulders. Devils and other animals were torturing people in all imaginable ways; and people were also torturing each other.

As I neared the doorway to this sinister scene, I felt a sucking sensation drawing me in like a whirlpool, and I found myself "flying" above the miserable landscape. The smell was putrid and the heat was almost unbearable but a part of me was fascinated by the seemingly infinite varieties of pain and anguish that was being inflicted on the inhabitants of this realm. Most of me wanted to leave so I had no difficulty and my feeling was that anyone could leave if they wished. I felt that no one or nothing had put those people in captivity except their belief in the agony they continued to suffer. I "flew" back to the doorway which was clearly visible from everywhere in the "Hell." I left with nothing but joy, but I still had a sense of myself as apart from that joy.

The next doorway in the tunnel wasn't much better. As far as the eye could see people walked on barren yellow ground with their heads down, completely engrossed in their own depressed self-pitying thoughts, unaware that anyone else was around them. A great feeling of loneliness and isolation emanated from the scene, and I shied away from getting too close, although no sucking sensation was felt near this opening in the cloud tunnel.

I flew along further up the tunnel and glanced in other doorways but the next one that made a lasting impression on me was a world of almost indescribable beauty. I looked upon a beautiful wooded garden with fountains and waterfalls and streams and bridges that glowed and sparkled with iridescent colors. A close depiction of the beauty of this world has been captured by the artist Gilbert Williams, whose work I discovered several years after my NDE. A feeling of peace and harmony flowed from this scene and I moved toward the doorway with a great desire to enter. As I began to go through the opening, my "nose" encountered what felt like plastic wrap webbing. I pushed forward but was gently rebuffed and a voice said, "You do not have the information to enter this world". At the time, I remember feeling disappointed but not judged as unworthy, just uninformed.

I then turned my attention to the light that was glowing around the fork to the right. I entered into the light, and was transformed by a feeling of utter absolute joy. There was nothing but joy. I said to the light "I'm here", and the light said "Great" in a voice that rang with happiness and bliss. I gave myself up to the bliss and learned many things that sound corny when described but are truths for me that resonate through me now and forever. I learned that I am eternal and though I may experience many forms of death, I will always know who I am. I have nothing to fear, only more to experience and I am the one that ultimately chooses what I experience. It sounds hokey but believe me it feels really, really good to know these things inside yourself. Eventually, I became disenchanted with eternal bliss and decided to leave. I said to the light "I'm leaving" and the light said "Great" continuing it's utter joyous and blissful existence unaltered in anyway by my presence.

I floated back down the tunnel glancing about me in continued wonder eventually settling on the threshold of a doorway that looked into outer space. Pieces of rock floated by and in the distance planets and galaxies spun and whirled. A rather conflicting feeling of both serenity and adventure surrounded me as I gazed upon the silent scene. The entrance to the tunnel was nearby and I could hear voices shouting "Don't go Sarah! What about Zane?" (My son who was five at the time of this incident). I grew annoyed at these voices because I wasn't intending to "go" anywhere and of course I was going to be there to watch Zane grow up. Another being appeared beside me and we "talked" about my options. We heard a voice say "If you pass through this door, you can't come back."

My next conscious memory was of lying in a hospital bed with uncountable tubes sticking into me and a respirator tube in my mouth. I was full of joy and humming with power although I was unable to move any part of my body of my own volition. I was also full of pain and that sensation quickly oriented me to my physical self again.

I have had to face many trials and challenges since my NDE including complete loss of identity, disability, poverty, loss of friends due to their inability to understand how the experience changed me, and chronic pain; but the knowledge of the eternity of my spirit and the freedom from the fear of death have created in me a foundation of peace that no temporary physical condition can shake. I have a great wish, that everyone could experience the wonders I have without having to suffer the trauma I did, for it would transform the world.

23. 'Help me, I don't want to die!

I grew up in a rational family with educated parents. My middle-class parents were critical of all religions. I was raised with the belief that death is an eternal sleep without dreams. In my childhood, I was sexually abused by family members. As a result of this trauma, I needed child psychiatry. I was chronically depressed and suicidal. In spite of all the concern and love of the doctors and nurses, I failed to overcome my trauma. When I was seventeen, I cut a main artery on the inside of my elbow. Blood spurted out to the ceiling in rhythm with my heartbeat. I felt lucky that at last I would sleep for eternity; never having to feel pain again or ever being a bother to anyone in the world again. I sank away into a dark depth.

Suddenly, I saw a scene from above and in a corner of the ceiling. I saw a room full of blood with a girl lying on the bed. Upon entering the room, the nurse began to scream. I couldn't understand what the panic was about. Everything was good and I felt peaceful. The doctor came in and the girl was laid on a stretcher. They pushed it hurriedly through the halls of the hospital. I floated along, like a balloon above the stretcher.

The doctor stopped in the big hospital hall and asked himself if they should immediately go to the operating room. High in the hall shone a warm golden, yellow light. Slowly but surely, I was being sucked toward the light. The doctor gently struck my face and called my name. Then I realized then that the girl on the stretcher was me. I got super-excited saying to myself, 'I'm in death, this is death!' I couldn't bear the thought that people on Earth don't understand death and that we go on living but without a body. I wanted to tell all the people on Earth that death isn't death and that there is more. But

I kept moving further from the Earth and toward the light. I looked towards the Earth and had compassion for all people. I felt sorrow for them, that they didn't know. That they were ignorant as they suffered and argued on earth.

Suddenly, I felt an emptiness and anxiety. I wondered where was I going once I was in the light? I began to panic and zoomed in to the ear of the doctor. I shouted from the depths of my soul, 'Help me, I don't want to die! Help me please!' That fraction of time of doubt near the doctor seemed like an eternity. I wanted him to save my life. I knew that once I was in the light, I would never be able to return to my body. I didn't want that, because my work on Earth was not finished. Although I didn't know what my work was or how I might complete it. Something very big was with me, understood me and brought me back.

Through this experience I became convinced that there is life after death. Unfortunately, I had not fully processed my trauma. After receiving child psychiatry, I continued receiving adult psychiatry. During this time, I had anorexia, took heroin, and prostituted myself. From a fellow patient, I became pregnant with twins. I felt I would not be a good mother for my children. I felt the emptiness again; I will go back into the Light so that the world will be better off without me. This time, I took an overdose of heroin and cocaine. I was found and paramedics began trying to reanimate me after a cardiac arrest.

With great speed, I was sucked downward into a dark void. The speed slowed and I became aware that this was because I was being resuscitation while going through a great mass of unfortunate, angry and mean souls. They wanted to keep me there. But each time my heart was resuscitated, with a hard shock I was back in my body. If they stopped resuscitation for even a few seconds, I was back in the dark void with the unfortunate souls. I kept thinking, 'Please don't stop resuscitating me.'

After waking up from this hellish experience during my coma, I turned my whole life around. This experience convinced me that the soul, after this life goes to a place I had earned by the things I had done during my life. I realized suddenly that this is my life and only I am responsible for how I handle things that come my way. I didn't always choose what comes my way, but I do choose how I deal with situations.

I immediately quit all medication, drugs, tobacco, self-mutilation, and the world of psychiatry. I began studying and went to work in the healthcare sector. I've been happily married now for sixteen years with a man who adopted my twins and together we had three more children. In concluding this story, I can say that I have reached my goal. I am fortunate and try to divide this good fortune to others. I can feel and spread unconditional love, because ultimately, all we take with us is what we have given.

24. JACKIE'S NDE

I was about 7 years old. I woke up feeling as if lead weights were on my stomach. I told my Dad I felt sick to my stomach. After a few minutes, I sat up and vomited large quantities of blood. My Dad helped me into the bathroom. It had been dark in my room and he hadn't realized I had thrown up blood until I threw up again. At that point, in the bathroom I felt myself pass out. I remember I wasn't concerned about falling, I think because my Dad was holding me up, plus I had never fainted before, so I didn't know what fainting was about!

I remember a bit about a car ride to the hospital. Then I remember the nurses trying to get me to drink this grape flavored stuff (barium?) so that they could take an X-ray, but I kept gagging. They told me that I was not allowed to throw the stuff up. I tried hard not to, while they kept pouring it down my throat. But I couldn't control the nausea, and again, I threw up a large amount of blood. I guess it was then that they realized my parents had not been exaggerating when they told them about how much blood I had already vomited. They stopped trying to take the X-ray (and forcing me to drink the grape stuff.) I was aware of them running by my side while they were taking me down the hall on a gurney to another room. I woke up for a bit to see that the doctor had already stretched one arm out on a board of some sort and was inserting a needle into it. I turned a bit to see the same thing in my other arm. I remember the doctor telling me something; maybe words of encouragement?

The next thing I knew, I was floating above myself. I could see my parents on the other side of the curtain on the bed next to me. My Mom was smoking a cigarette; and my Dad looked very stressed, had his hands folded on his lap. I could sort of see myself, but mostly I was watching my parents (as a 7 year old would.) I don't remember having a body when I was above myself.

I could see my body, but couldn't see the me who was above the scene, up in the air doing the looking. Then, every time after that, when I tried to open my eyes, it was grainy and noisy, just like when cable goes out on your TV; same sound and visual. My first memory after that was being back in my body, waking up enough to know my Mom was there. She told me if I lay quietly, she would read to me. I remember drifting in and out. I stayed in the hospital for a week.

In my early 20's, when I was having an ulcer problem, I found out more about what had happened, and why. They did an upper GI, which showed that my jugular vein was misshapen; probably due to the fact that I have always liked to sleep with my hand curled up under my chin. The doctor said he thought that years of sleeping like that, with the gentle pressure of my finger resting on my throat, had trained my jugular vein to bend into an abnormal position; a bit too close to my esophagus. This resulted in the piece of glass that I had swallowed nicking my jugular vein as it cut the inside of my throat.

Another thing: several years later, I was telling my Mom about my experience. She told me that soon after she lit the cigarette, the doctor yelled at her to put it out. But she kept smoking, ignoring the doctor, until a nurse said to her, "Put it out NOW - or LEAVE! There are oxygen tanks present, and they could ignite!"

THEN, my Mom put the cigarette out; but she was embarrassed, she said, that she was yelled at by the doctor; and that she had buckled under their pressure to put the cigarette out (she is very strong willed!). She also told me that the point at which she had lit the cigarette was when the doctor had ordered more blood. The nurse had said, "Do you want it stat?" and his response was "Stat, hell! You run, and you run fast...she is already dead...but we can maybe bring her around if we get more blood into her quick enough!" That's when my Mom lit up her cigarette, she said. I said to my Mom, "That's when I was floating above myself, and I saw everything you just told me, happening just the way you said it." We went on to corroborate other details of what I had seen. She was really scared and unnerved about this, because we shared the same memories of what had happened; and that was the same point that the doctor had just told the nurse I was dead.

25. GINA'S NDE

During the car accident, I can remember feeling and sensing my body rolling with the car. I remember flying through the air and landing softly on the ground. The whole time I felt like I was watching a movie. After I landed on the ground, I remember thinking that I should scream, so I screamed a slow, calm scream. I remember being in intensive care before the surgery, and a man of the cloth (that's all I know as there was no face, just a presence) took my hand and told me I would be all right after the surgery. When he took my hand, energy passed from him to me. I could feel it go through my whole body. I wouldn't let go of his hand, so he gently pried my hand off his.

The next thing I knew, I was passing through a tunnel towards a very peaceful and beautiful bright light. I was met by moving forms that were pure energy. It was such a beautiful, loving place. I remember loving it there, and feeling astounded by the love that I was receiving. I reviewed my life, and I did the judging. I went back to when I was about two years old. I know I was given all types of information, but now I don't remember just what it was. But sometimes, I just know things and I don't know how I know them. It's almost as if I have an additional sense.

I had no choice but to return; I didn't want to and I begged to stay. I was told that I had much to do before I could return.

When I came back, there was an angel, a glowing bright light, at the foot of my bed. It stayed there as I recovered. As my health improved, the light faded and became more distant.

I was very upset that I had to come back. In fact, I thought it was because I was such an awful person that even God did not want me.

I told no one of this experience until I was in my thirties, after seeing an interview with James Moody.

26. JOANNA' NDE

Let me tell you a bit about myself before I begin. I am a forty-six year old woman now. I live alone with my dog and my cat. I have multiple disabilities that keep me at home most of the time. My days are either Good Days or Bad Days, depending how my disabilities are affecting me. I live with some manner of chronic pain every day, from the time I wake up until the time I go to bed. I am stubborn, so I refuse to give in to the pain or illness, and I just live the best and fullest way I can for that day. I have a home health aide that comes here twice a week. She is young, so I end up redoing most of her work, but she is getting better as time goes on. My daughter is going to be twenty-four this month and is making a good life for herself since she left an abusive husband a few months ago. My existence today is due to her need for me as she grew up. There is no other reason am I here today. In the past, suicide was something I had planned, right down to the time I was going to do it. I knew that as soon as she was on her own with her life stable to the point that she no longer needed me, I was going to put an end to my life. I got a lesson I would like to share with you. I do hope it helps someone.

I started being ill in the early 1980s. Physically, it started about 1983 with my insides. Around 1985 I was hospitalized after I became unable to stand or walk due to a back injury I received playing softball in 1981. I was told I might never walk again. I was divorced at the time and trying to raise my daughter. I ended up never being able to hold on to a job, due to one illness or another. I found myself on welfare, unable to work at all. As the years passed, my illnesses got worse.

In 1987, I lost forty-five pounds in about a three-month period. No doctor could find out what was wrong with me. I was finally diagnosed in the early 1990s and was told there was no cure or surgery that could help me. Not much is known about what I have, so I must live life as best as I can. Medication has not helped. I tell you that so that when I talk about being depressed, you will understand how and why I reached the depths of wanting to take my own life. I came to know a lot of humiliation due to my illness. Being as young as I was and not being able to live a normal life made me feel like I would never have love in my life. So once my daughter moved out on her own, I would be alone. There is nobody that is going to want someone with even ONE of the problems I have, never mind all of them.

In 1992, I was taken to the hospital in an ambulance. I was informed in the emergency room that I was having a heart attack. The doctor and nurses were a little surprised at that, because I was only thirty-seven, I was white, and I was female without high blood pressure or high cholesterol. All of a sudden, I started crying because I did not want to die - death was starting to scare me. In the intensive care unit, relatives came and went. I had not realize what bad shape I was in. My ex-husband showed up in the room with my daughter. He told me not to worry about my daughter, because he and his wife would take good care of her because they did love her. That is all I remember of the visit. As my ex-husband was telling me that, I was watching what looked like a white coating starting to cover the door I was facing. It was moving from the bottom upward. It slowly covered the whole area so that everything I could see was of the cleanest, purest white I had ever seen in my entire life. My daughter has told me that at the time when she was there with her father, she had thought I had fallen asleep - but all of a sudden she heard the heart machine beep a long sound, and the line was flat across. They stepped back, as a team of about five people gathered around me, telling each other things to do and to get. They closed the curtain, and then she saw someone go in to me with the machine to paddle my chest. They were asked to wait in the waiting area. They were escorted out of my room and were told that someone would be out to the waiting area to tell them what was going on as soon as they could.

Meanwhile, I was engulfed by the best feeling I had ever had in my life. I was continuing further and further, deeper and deeper, into that feeling of where I was. Never had I seen or even imagined a place of such purity and peace. Serenity, tranquillity, and a calm I had never known before were present there. I could tell there was no illness, no pain or suffering of any kind there. Nothing at all negative was anywhere in the area. Nothing bad or evil. The more I looked, around the better things seemed to become. I do remember feeling, and of saying aloud, "Awe!" because I was awestruck. As I looked ahead, I saw the softest whiteness I had ever seen. It was spread out as far as my eyes could see. It seemed to go on for miles in length and width. I was amazed and kept looking ahead, and I started to see a light bluish-gray color in the bottom of the soft whiteness. As I drifted on, I started to make out that the color I could see was really the silhouettes of many people together. Big, small, young, old - no one was of any race, because they were all silhouettes. There were many of them there. So many that I was not able to count them. There was a sense of unconditional love all around.

I wanted to continue. I wanted to know what this place was. I wanted to belong to it. As I got close to them, it seemed like a white fog was being lifted in order for me to see better and more clearly. At about that time, I was being approached by what appeared to be a woman. She came close enough to me to take my hand. I do know I felt love for her as soon as I set eyes on her. I got a feeling that she was loving and accepting of me, too. All the other people stayed where they were. They looked as if they were talking with one another. I do know that the woman and I talked for a while, but I do not remember what we said. Then I was opening my eyes, and my head was tipped towards the floor. I was trying to raise my head to see where I was, but my head was too much at an angle for me to lift it up. I looked to my right and there stood a stranger I had never seen before. He said, "Hi! You must not be comfortable like that. I will put your head up for you." Then he said, "You gave us quite a scare, young lady." The man was the doctor that had gotten my heart started again. I remember not wanting to talk. I felt very sad and empty. I was confused. I closed my eyes because I wanted to go back to the feeling I had just been having. I wanted the whiteness and everything else that was there. But when I closed my eyes, it did not work.

27. ELLEN'S NDE

I was admitted to the hospital for a routine repeat C-section. I recall being put under and deep sleep...other words, no recollections. Then, I heard the anaesthesiologist calling out my blood pressure.

His voice was calm and deliberate. Suddenly, I materialized at the ceiling, to the right of my body. I saw my body and knew it was mine. I saw the surgeon. He was listening to some country western music, and suturing my body ~~beginning from the left he was progressing to the right. He was Asian and I found it interesting his choice of music. Everything was in color. I looked at the body several times and knew it was mine but I felt complete objectivity with it. I asked (within my own thoughts) if I was hungry or need anything; no. It was wonderful where I was! I had no problems or cares. Listening to the dropping blood pressure, I knew the body was going to die if I did not return; it was not a concern of mine. Then, I heard the following: "25........."

Suddenly, I was plunged downward, almost like being sucked into some vortex. Everything was black. There was absolutely no light. After a while, I saw a distant light. I was curious about the light. I felt myself being moved steadily forward to ward the light. When I was about 30-50 feet away, I noticed the light appeared to be flames coming from inside a doorway. There was a dark, ominous figure to the right of the outer door frame. He appeared evil. His right hand kept beckoning me inward in kind of a rolling hand motion. I became very afraid. Sounds like soul wrenching screams (not screams of pain, but screams of the soul), emitted from the fire behind him. I tried to pull back but discovered I could not.

On either side of me, there appeared "soul-guides." Their guidance provided the energy that kept me moving forward. I continued to try to pull back but discovered, as I had no physical form, I had nothing to pull back with. I felt like a huge magnet was steadily pulling me into the room/the fire. I started screaming, "Let me die." I knew I was talking about the impossible; I was asking to let my soul die. Repeatedly, I screamed, "Let me die," as it was preferable to entering the doorway.

I knew I was back in my body but I did not want to be there. I wanted to be in the first place above everything. The doctors and nurses were shaking me and calling me by name. Now, I think, I had a voice. I kept calling out, let me die. I could hear the sounds in the room and knew they were trying to revive me, wanted me to return. Finally, one voice said, "You have a boy." I replied, "Eighteen more years then I can go."

The next morning, the anaesthesiologist came to my room. He looked deep into my eyes and asked me if "there was anything I remembered." I nodded my head up and down. He asked if I "wanted to discuss" it; I violently shook my head, no. Sombrely, he told he would answer any questions for me when I was ready. I just looked at him.

In 1983, I was pregnant again. Scared because of my experience in 1981, and afraid they would not get me back to care for my children, I spoke with a doctor. He listened to me. Then, he got my medical records. As he was reading the reports, he kept shaking his head and saying, "Oh, no. Oh, no." His response confirmed for me the medical aspect of what had happened. I asked," what was the bottom number? 25 over what?" He said, "The blackness was 25 over zero."

The doctor (who reviewed my records at a later date), believed it was the aesthetic that was used. This was not a bad dream; it was so real that my blood pressure fell drastically. That aesthetic is not currently on the market, so I am told. I THOUGHT it was something called, "Kennington" but it could have been Ketamine. He did tell me that many, many people had been experience with "bad dreams."

Please understand that I do not need confirmation of the incident happening. I am rather awed by the experience. I changed my life tremendously as I became keenly aware of the presence/existence of God, and my accountability with him is very clear!

28. LISA B's NDE

I was doing veterinary work on a horse. The horse reared up and struck me directly with its front hoof hitting my head, face and arm, as I tried to protect myself. I fractured several facial bones, detached retina, and fractured radius in arm. Was unconscious for a brief period. My experience during this period, however, seemed to take much more 'time', if it were to occur strictly in this physical dimension.

I found myself suddenly above my body, looking down on the whole scene. I could see things that were outside the stall that I was in even though that would have been impossible if I was seeing from where my body was. It was like looking down like a camera that has pulled up to see an expanded view of a scene. I became aware that there were 2 (possibly 3) 'beings' with me, one on either side. They were communicating with me directly, telepathically, just putting their input directly into my consciousness. No words and much less 'time'. I knew I was somehow removed from these usual 'laws' or ways of processing experience. While I did not sense a life review on specific terms, I was shown, by understanding; not pictures or movies; many significant things in my life. The good and the bad. All focused on my contributions; how I handled myself. I remember the almost palpable absence of all fear. I was made to understand that this fear is what underlies many of our poor choices. That there is nothing to fear.

I felt compassion toward myself like I never could imagine possible. A type of love that I never knew. Empathy, sympathy for all I'd experienced and a new determination to let myself live as I could and should and must. I knew I had a clear purpose and was shown this purpose so I could understand how needed I was. I felt no pain. Not sure if I had a body or if my guides did. It didn't seem to matter. I was in contact with all information; total understanding of everything. But what I connected with was just the importance of my life purpose. I saw the future (don't remember it now) and even saw how difficult recovery would be from the accident, but knew I would get through it, which was all that mattered for me to get on to do what I am meant to do.

And that I could only serve this purpose, if I lost my fears; of rejection, not being liked for the stands I took, other people having control of things (only we do), etc. And then I could act out of pure love; no complications or compromises. Once I 'understood all this', I found myself back in my body in excruciating pain. I also had the knowledge that these guides are always there when they are needed. They are the ultimate nurturers.

29. RACHEL F's NDE

When I was 20, I went into early labor with my first baby. After 4 difficult days, I was given an episiotomy from which I lost a huge amount of blood. Two days after my daughter was born, it was decided that a blood transfusion would be started.

Roughly two hours into the transfusion I felt I needed to use the toilet and hauled myself up, dragging the bag of blood beside me. Never before or after this experience, have I felt so very weak and floaty. It was a great effort to move.

I shuffled myself back from the toilet to the ward and slowly and carefully lay myself down. The ward was empty except for one other new mother who lay opposite me. I smiled at her and realized I was shivering. I have always felt the cold, so at the time, assumed I just needed to warm up. I tried to lay still for a moment and quickly realized my whole body was shaking. The woman opposite me asked me if I was ok. I tried to tell her yes and that I was just cold but my teeth had begun to chatter and my jaw felt too stiff to control, instead, I nodded, still not at all understanding at all, why I was tremoring.

I reached for my buzzer to ask a midwife for an extra blanket. As soon as she saw me she pressed a button behind me and within a few seconds I was surrounded. The transfusion was immediately stopped. I saw the woman opposite me staring at me, I was acutely aware of how scared she looked and the curtain being drawn around her.

I wanted to ask what was happening, but I could not soften my jaw to speak and almost immediately an oxygen mask was placed on my face. I remember fighting for breath. I remember how hard my chest was thumping. My thoughts seemed scattered, my eyes somewhat frantic and when I noticed my fingernails turning blue I very calmly, internally thought to myself 'Oh, I'm dying.' It was very matter of fact with a hint of 'oops'.

I tried to keep myself calm internally. I was talking to myself in my mind, thinking of my family, trying to gain strength from thinking of them. I remember feeling frustrated, annoyed that they weren't there with me, that I couldn't tell them goodbye.

I tried to keep my eyes open but suddenly felt so very tired. My eyes were so heavy, so I let them rest and then I was up.

I briefly hovered over my newborn baby, hoped she'd remember me, then I was travelling.

It felt like I was shooting through a tunnel, but I couldn't see any sides to it. It was dark, but illuminated. I was not alone; I could sense a presence with me. I was tumbling, forward/upward at an unfathomable speed. It felt like wind. All throughout me. Inside of me. I likened it at that age to being on a rollercoaster, that rushing feeling. It was wonderful. I felt so light, so free. Simultaneously, I experienced this fully and watched myself experience this with clear vision from a little distance. I can still see myself tumbling if I concentrate on the memory.

This travelling went on for some time until I became aware that I was in a new place. Like a room without walls, without a ceiling, without a floor. I had 360-degree vision and could see all around me. Again, there was darkness, but I did not feel afraid. Again, I felt a presence, and also felt complete trust in this company. A 'movie' for want of a better word, began to play. It was black and white and huge. As if I were staring at a giant screen that filled the whole of every which way I turned. The 'movie' was my life from birth to death, every minute of it, every event I had ever experienced. I watched it and I relived it. It was at this point I realized Time did no longer appear to me as it had in my body. It was as if I were projected into a moment, or dragged through time, backwards before forwards, to re-feel. I witnessed at this point, the sexual abuse I had experienced and suppressed as a young child, as well as out of body experiences I had at this time and at night when I was lying in my bed. I could see myself flying out of body and I remembered. It was at this point I also saw and recalled a guide that had been with me throughout my growing. While watching/re-experiencing each moment, I found I was now able to experience each event through the emotions of all present at each time.

I watched my own poor mistakes and learnt from every re-living. I watched myself as a child, bitten by a guinea-pig and in shock, half launch it onto the sofa. I felt shame at this time. Because I felt the fear of the guinea-pig. No one condemned me. I was asked only, what I had learnt. I was comforted at this time. Consoled and reassured. I had learnt so much. How big an impact my seemingly small actions had on a large scale. How my choices and behavior rippled through the lives of countless others. How the Love I showed spread like wildfire. How the way I mistreated others, deeply hurt and affected them and also how that pain, fear and confusion would then impact the lives of others too. In the 'time' I spent in this re-living, I developed a deep gratitude for many things. The experience of life for one. The people and the hearts that had touched my soul in beautiful ways and the fragility of being human. My new found wisdom seemed satisfactory and we were moving.

Again, we travelled through the illuminated darkness until I saw a pinpoint of light in the distance. When I saw it, it was like a remembering. I knew where I was headed and I wanted to get there, fast. I can't recall if I was moving myself towards it or if I was being 'drawn' to it somehow but it was a 'need/desire' within me.

We moved faster and faster toward this beam of light. It grew in size in my vision, in intensity. I felt like I was flying.

We burst into it. And it was indescribable.

It was every incredible feeling that I will never be able to describe. It was immediate peace. Absolute, whole peace all throughout me. There was no pain, there was no fear, there was no shame. I felt completely accepted. Totally whole and loved. Loved beyond comprehension. Loved in my entirety. Loved with a Love I have not felt here. Loved with the purest love there can be.

I felt I was 'home'. I felt I knew this place/space/being. It was light. It filled every space of my 360d vision. It had no form that I can recall, which for a long time left me with other questions but it was beautiful, and not blinding in the slightest.

It was as if I 'merged' with the light, it absorbed me, I absorbed it, we became One, completely. In these moments, I learnt much. About our existence as humans, about our planet and what we as a species need to do to resolve its problems, the healing that our planet and us as people need.

I was communicating with the light as well as experiencing being within it and One with it. A conversation began, using telepathy I assume and I was asked if I would like to return. The absolute truth of my soul is that I felt completely insulted at this suggestion. I was horrified at the thought and felt myself loud within me, respond No! There was a pause and I felt a little confused, wondering why this was being asked of me. Again, the same question repeated within me, 'Do you wish to go back?' Again, I said No. There was another pause and then I was shown the baby I had just birthed, lying in the crib beside my body. I was shown much from time to come. Various outcomes that depended solely on whether or not I returned to my body. There would be countless lives that would be touched with this Love if I returned and many that would not know it if I did not. I remember taking what can only be described as a deep, soul sigh. A knowing sigh. An understanding.

Immediately after seeing this, and holding the vision of my newborn daughter in my 'sight', her possible future if I stayed, I said 'Yes'.

I asked for a moment more and I was granted it. I soaked all the love I could into my entire being. It felt glorious. I felt pure and light and whole and loved and loved and loved. In this 'moment' I understood everything. Creation, purpose, love. Physics, numbers, existence. I was completely at One with all of existence.

And then I was shooting backwards and it was cold and dark and I was grieving the light before I even hit my body.

It was another 2 days before I could hold my baby. I spent 48 hours lying naked as the day I was born, in and out of consciousness. I couldn't speak. I just lay there and cried quietly. I hurt, everywhere. I felt trapped, restricted, lonely. I missed the light, the love, immediately and immensely.

It took my spirit longer to recover than my body, though that in itself was a long time. I was very depressed, for many years, and often dealt with suicidal thoughts because the desire to be 'home' was so great. I was confused for the longest time. I was afraid, I found being in a body painful, restricting and limiting. I am still greatly uncomfortable with it; however, I have learned to love and be grateful for my life and breath.

I was at my father's bedside when he passed on 7 years after my NDE when many pieces seemed to fit into place in my mind. I started meditating at this time and rapidly forced myself to recover. From the sexual abuse, the loss of my greatest friend (my father) and excruciating loss of light.

I remembered my purpose at this time. I started an online community called 'Bruised But Not Broken' and over the following 6 years built a community of over 700,000 individuals that had experienced sexual abuse, trauma, addiction, loss. Together, we work to heal our wounds and strive to be the best version of ourselves we can be.

Since this time, I have also published two books. One relevant to my sexual abuse and healing, the other relevant to my Near Death Experience and time spent with the light and my higher self.

My NDE was without doubt, the most incredible and transformative experience of my life. I have never forgotten a single moment of it and doubt I ever will. It took me time, but I allowed it to transform me in the most beautiful of ways and I try every day to live and love the way I was loved in those very sacred moments.

Near-Death Experiences Evidence for Their Reality

Near-death experiences (NDEs) are reported by about 17% of those who nearly die. NDEs have been reported by children, adults, scientists, physicians, priests, ministers, among the religious and atheists, and from countries throughout the world.

While no two NDEs are the same, there are characteristic features that are commonly observed in NDEs. These characteristics include a perception of seeing and hearing apart from the physical body, passing into or through a tunnel, encountering a mystical light, intense and generally positive emotions, a review of part or all of their prior life experiences, encountering deceased loved ones, and a choice to return to their earthly life.

Methods

There is no uniformly accepted definition of near-death experience. Definitions of NDE with some variability have been used throughout the 35 plus years that NDE has been the subject of scholarly investigation. For my retrospective investigations, an NDE was required to have both a near-death and experience component.

Individuals were considered to be "near-death" if they were so physically compromised that if their condition did not improve they would be expected to irreversibly die. Near-death experiencers (NDErs) included in my investigations were generally unconscious and may have required cardiopulmonary resuscitation. The "experience" component of an NDE had to occur when they were near death. Also, the experience had to be reasonably lucid, which excluded fragmentary or brief disorganized memories. For an experience to be classified as an NDE, there had to be a score of seven or above on the NDE Scale. The NDE Scale asks 16 questions about the NDE content and is the most validated scale to help distinguish NDEs from other types of experiences.

In 1998, a website called the Near Death Experience Research Foundation (NDERF, nderf.org) was established to conduct NDE research and to be a public service. It is NDERF policy that all NDE accounts shared with NDERF are posted on the website if the NDErs give permission to do so. Nearly all NDErs allow their experiences to be posted on the NDERF website. Portions of the NDERF website, including the NDE questionnaire, have been posted in over 20 different languages. The NDERF website has consistently been at or near the top of websites listed from a Google search for the term "near-death experiences." This prominence of the NDERF website provided a unique opportunity to conduct a large-scale study of NDEs, including NDEs from around the world. At the current time there are over 3,700 NDEs posted on the NDERF website, which is by far the largest collection of publicly accessible NDE accounts in the world.

The NDERF website has a form allowing near-death experiencers to share a detailed narrative of their experiences, and includes a detailed questionnaire. Extensive prior studies found that an Internet survey has validity that is equivalent to traditional pencil-and-paper survey. All experiences shared with the NDERF website are reviewed. Sequentially shared NDEs from the NDERF website were studied. NDEs included for study were single NDE accounts, shared in English, and were shared by the individual who personally had the NDE. An investigation of the NDEs shared with NDERF led to nine lines of evidence suggesting the reality of NDE.

Results Suggesting the Reality of Near-Death Experiences

Line of Evidence #1

Lucid, organized experiences while unconscious, comatose, or clinically dead

Near-death experiences occur at a time when the person is so physically compromised that they are typically unconscious, comatose, or clinically dead. Considering NDEs from both a medical perspective and logically, it should not be possible for unconscious people to often report highly lucid experiences that are clear and logically structured. Most NDErs report supernormal consciousness at the time of their NDEs.

The NDERF survey asked, "How did your highest level of consciousness and alertness during the experience compare to your normal, everyday consciousness and alertness?" Of 1,122 NDErs surveyed, 835 (74.4%) indicated they had "More consciousness and alertness than normal"; 229 (20.4%) experienced "Normal consciousness and alertness"; and only 58 (5.2%) had "Less consciousness and alertness than normal."

The NDERF survey also asks, "If your highest level of consciousness and alertness during the experience was different from your normal everyday consciousness and alertness, please explain." In response to this question, NDErs commonly reported that consciousness during their experiences was "clear", "more aware", and often associated with heightened awareness.

Near-death experiences often occur in association with cardiac arrest. Prior studies found that 10–20 seconds following cardiac arrest, electroencephalogram measurements generally find no significant measureable brain cortical electrical activity. A prolonged, detailed, lucid experience following cardiac arrest should not be possible, yet this is reported in many NDEs. This is especially notable given the prolonged period of amnesia that typically precedes and follows recovery from cardiac arrest.

Line of Evidence #2

Seeing ongoing events from a location apart from the physical body while unconscious (out-of-body experience)

A common characteristic of near-death experiences is an out-of-body experience. An out-of-body experience (OBE) is the apparent separation of consciousness from the body. About 45% of near-death experiencers report OBEs which involves them seeing and often hearing ongoing earthly events from a perspective that is apart, and usually above, their physical bodies. Following cardiac arrest, NDErs may see, and later accurately describe, their own resuscitation.

The first prospective study of the accuracy of out-of-body observations during near-death experiences was by Dr. Michael Sabom. This study investigated a group of patients who had cardiac arrests with NDEs that included OBEs, and compared them with a control group of patients who experienced cardiac crises but did not have NDEs. Both groups of patients were asked to describe their own resuscitation as best they could. Sabom found that the group of NDE patients were much more accurate than the control group in describing their own resuscitations.

"A man should look for what is, and not what he thinks should be."

-Albert Einstein

Another prospective study of out-of-body observations during near-death experiences with similar methodology to Sabom's study was published by Dr. Penny Sartori. This study also found that near-death experiencers were often remarkably accurate in describing details of their own resuscitations. The control group that did not have NDEs was highly inaccurate and often could only guess at what occurred during their resuscitations.

Two large retrospective studies investigated the accuracy of out-of-body observations during near-death experiences. The first was by Dr. Janice Holden. Dr. Holden reviewed NDEs with OBEs in all previously published scholarly articles and books, and found 89 case reports. Of the case reports reviewed, 92% were considered to be completely accurate with no inaccuracy whatsoever when the OBE observations were later investigated.

Another large retrospective investigation of near-death experiences that included out-of-body observations was recently published. This study was a review of 617 NDEs that were sequentially shared on the NDERF website. Of these NDEs, there were 287 NDEs that had OBEs with sufficient information to allow objective determination of the reality of their descriptions of their observations during the OBEs. Review of the 287 OBEs found that 280 (97.6%) of the OBE descriptions were entirely realistic and lacked any content that seemed unreal. In this group of 287 NDErs with OBEs, there were 65 (23%) who personally investigated the accuracy of their own OBE observations after recovering from their life-threatening event. Based on these later investigations, none of these 65 OBErs found any inaccuracy in their own OBE observations.

The high percentage of accurate out-of-body observations during near-death experiences does not seem explainable by any possible physical brain function as it is currently known. This is corroborated by OBEs during NDEs that describe accurate observations while they were verifiably clinically comatose. Further corroboration comes from the many NDEs that have been reported with accurate OBE observations of events occurring far from their physical body, and beyond any possible physical sensory awareness. Moreover, NDE accounts have been reported with OBEs that accurately observed events that were completely unexpected by the NDErs. This further argues against NDEs as being a result of illusory memories originating from what the NDErs might have expected during a close brush with death.

Line of Evidence #3

Near-death experiences with vision in the blind and supernormal vision

There have been a few case reports of near-death experiences in the blind. The largest study of this was by Dr. Kenneth Ring. This Investigation included 31 blind or substantially visually impaired individuals who had NDEs or out-of-body experiences. Of the 31 individuals in the study, 10 were not facing life-threatening events at the time of their experiences, and thus their experiences were not NDEs. There were 14 individuals who were blind from birth in this study, and nine of them described vision during their experiences. This investigation presented case reports of those born totally blind that described in NDEs that were highly visual with content consistent with typical NDEs.

The NDERF website has received additional case reports of near-death experiences among those legally blind. For illustration, the following NDE happened to Marta, a five-year-old blind girl who walked into a lake:

"I slowly breathed in the water and became unconscious. A beautiful lady dressed in bright white light pulled me out. The lady looked into my eyes asked me what I wanted. I was unable to think of anything until it occurred to me to travel around the lake. As I did so, I saw detail that I would not have seen in "real" life. I could go anywhere, even to the tops of trees, simply by my intending to go there. I was legally blind. For the first time I was able to see leaves on trees, bird's feathers, bird's eyes, details on telephone poles and what was in people's back yards. I was seeing far better than 20/20 vision.

An NDERF survey question asked 1,122 near-death experiencers, "Did your vision differ in any way from your normal, everyday vision (in any aspect, such as clarity, field of vision, colors, brightness, depth perception degree of solidness/transparency of objects, etc.)?" In response, 722 (64.3%) answered "Yes", 182 (16.2%) said "Uncertain", and 218 (19.4%) responded "No". A review of narrative responses to this question revealed that vision during NDEs was often apparently supernormal. Here are some illustrative examples from NDEs:

"Colors were beyond any I had ever seen."

"Everything seemed so much more colorful and brighter than normal."

"My vision was greatly increased. I was able to see things as close or as far as I needed. There was no strain involved it was almost like auto zooming a camera."

"I had 360 degree vision, I could see above, below, on my right, on my left, behind, I could see everywhere at the same time!"

Vision in near-death experiencers that are blind, including totally blind from birth, has been described in many case reports. This, along with the finding that vision in NDEs is usually different from normal everyday vision and often described as supernormal, further suggests that NDEs cannot be explained by our current understanding of brain function. This is also further evidence that NDEs are not a product of what NDErs would have expected to occur during a life-threatening event.

Line of Evidence #4

Near-death experiences that occur while under general anesthesia

Under adequate general anesthesia it should not be possible to have a lucid organized memory. Prior studies using EEG and functional imaging of the brains of patients under general anesthesia provide substantial evidence that the anesthetized brain should be unable to produce lucid memories. As previously discussed, following cardiac arrest the EEG becomes flat in 10 to 20 seconds, and there is usually amnesia prior to and following the arrest. The occurrence of a cardiac arrest while under general anesthesia is a combination of circumstances in which no memory from that time should be possible. Here is an illustrative example of an NDE that occurred under general anesthesia during surgery for a heart valve replacement:

"*During my surgery I felt myself lift from my body and go above the operating table. The doctor told me later that they had kept my heart open and stopped for a long time, and they had a great amount of difficulty getting my heart started again. That must have been when I left my body because I could see the doctors nervously trying to get my heart going. It was strange to be so detached from my physical body. I was curious about what they were doing but not concerned. Then, as I drifted farther away, I saw my father at the head of the table. He looked up at me, which did give me a surprise because he had been dead now for almost a year.*"

I reviewed 613 near-death experiences shared with NDERF, and found 23 NDEs that appeared to have occurred while under general anesthesia. Cardiac arrest was the most common life-threatening event that was described in association with the occurrence of these NDEs. I compared the responses of these 23 NDErs to the 590 non-anesthesia NDErs by reviewing how both groups responded to 33 survey questions that asked about the content of the NDEs. Chi-square statistics was used for this comparison. Due to the large number of questions asked, statistical significance was set at $p=0.01$. The only statistically significant difference between the two groups was that the anesthesia NDEs were more likely to describe tunnels in their experiences.

An NDERF survey question asked, "How did your highest level of consciousness and alertness during the experience compare to your normal everyday consciousness and alertness?" For the NDEs occurring under general anesthesia, 19 (83%) of the respondents answered, "More consciousness and alertness than normal," to this question, compared to 437 (74%) for all other NDEs. The responses to this question by the two groups were not statistically significantly different. This suggests, remarkably, that the level of consciousness and alertness in NDEs is not modified by general anesthesia.

Other near-death experience investigators have reported NDEs occurring while under general anesthesia. Dr. Bruce Greyson, a leading NDE researcher at the University of Virginia, states:

"In our collection of NDEs, 127 out of 578 NDE cases (22%) occurred under general anesthesia, and they included such features as OBEs that involved experiencers' watching medical personnel working on their bodies, an unusually bright or vivid light, meeting deceased persons, and thoughts, memories, and sensations that were clearer than usual."

NDEs due to cardiac arrest while under general anesthesia occur and are medically inexplicable.

Line of Evidence #5

Near-death experiences and life reviews

Some near-death experiences include a review of part or all of their prior lives. This NDE element is called a life review. NDErs typically describe their life review from a third-person perspective. The life review may include awareness of what others were feeling and thinking at the time earlier in their life when they interacted with them. This previously unknown awareness of what other people were feeling or thinking when they interacted with them is often surprising and unexpected to the NDErs. Here is an example of a life review: "

I went into a dark place with nothing around me, but I wasn't scared. It was really peaceful there. I then began to see my whole life unfolding before me like a film projected on a screen, from babyhood to adult life. It was so real! I was looking at myself, but better than a 3-D movie as I was also capable of sensing the feelings of the persons I had interacted with through the years. I could feel the good and bad emotions I made them go through."

In my review of 617 near-death experiences from NDERF, a life review occurred in 88 NDEs (14%). None of the life reviews in these

NDEs appeared to have any unrealistic content as determined by my review or based on comments by the NDErs about their own life reviews. Life reviews may include long forgotten details of their earlier life that the NDErs later confirm really happened. If NDEs were unreal experiences, it would be expected that there would be significant error in life reviews and possibly hallucinatory features. The consistent accuracy of life reviews, including the awareness of long-forgotten events and awareness of the thoughts and feelings of others from past interactions, further suggests the reality of NDEs.

Line of Evidence #6

Encountering deceased loved ones in near-death experiences

Near-death experiences may describe encounters with people that they knew during their earthly life. The following is an example of encountering a deceased loved ones in an NDE. This example is also notable as the NDEr was born totally deaf:

"I approached the boundary. No explanation was necessary for me to understand, at the age of ten, that once I cross[ed] the boundary, I could never come back— period. I was more than thrilled to cross. I intended to cross, but my ancestors over another boundary caught my attention. They were talking in telepathy, which caught my attention. I was born profoundly deaf and had all hearing family members, all of which knew sign language! I could read or communicate with about twenty ancestors of mine and others through telepathic methods. It overwhelmed me. I could not believe how many people I could telepathize with simultaneously.

When people known to the near-death experiencers are encountered in NDEs, the great majority are people who are deceased. A study by Dr. Emily Kelly was a comparison of 74 NDEs with descriptions of encountering deceased individuals with 200 NDEs that did not describe encounters with the deceased. This study found that when NDErs encountered beings known to them from their earthly lives in their NDEs, only 4% described meeting beings that were alive at the time of their experiences. I reviewed 84 NDEs from NDERF that described encounters with individual(s) that they knew in their earthly life. There were only three NDEs (4%) where the encountered beings were alive at the time of the NDEs, consistent with the findings of the Kelly study.

In dreams or hallucinations when familiar persons are present they are much more likely to be living and from recent memory. This is in sharp contrast to near-death experiencers where familiar persons encountered are almost always deceased. Cases have been reported by NDErs of seeing a person who they thought was living, but in fact had recently died. These cases illustrate that NDEs cannot be explained by the experiencer's expectation of what would happen during a life-threatening event. Further evidence that NDEs are not a result of expectation comes from the aforementioned Kelly study where in one-third of the cases the encountered deceased person had a poor or distant relationship with the NDEr, or was someone that had died before the NDEr was born.

Line of Evidence #7

Near-death experiences of young children

Investigation of near-death experiences in very young children is important because at an early age they are less likely to have established religious beliefs, cultural understandings about death, or even an awareness of what death is. Very young children would be very unlikely to have heard about near-death experiences or understand them. I investigated the NDEs in children age five and younger in the same group of 613 NDErs previously discussed in the section on NDEs while under general anesthesia. Two NDEs were excluded as they did not provide their age in the survey. The study groups included 26 NDErs that were age 5 and younger (average 3.6 years old) and 585 NDErs age 6 and older at the time of their NDEs. The NDERF survey included 33 questions about the content of their NDEs. Chi-square statistics was used to compare the responses to these 33 questions between the two groups. There was no statistically significant difference to the responses between the two groups to any of the 33 questions. The NDERF study found that the content of NDEs in children age five and younger appeared to be the same as the content of NDEs in older children and adults. The finding of the NDERF study are corroborated by the investigation of Dr. Cherie Sutherland who reviewed thirty years of scholarly literature regarding the NDEs of children and concluded:

"It has often been supposed that the NDEs of very young children will have a content limited to their vocabulary. However, it is now clear that the age of children at the time of their NDE does not in any way determine its complexity. Even prelinguistic children have later reported quite complex experiences.... Age does not seem in any way to affect the content of the NDE."

Very young children have near-death experience content that is strikingly similar to older children and adults. This is further evidence that NDEs are occurring independently of pre-existing cultural beliefs, religious training, or awareness of the existence of NDE.

Line of Evidence #8

Cross-cultural study of near-death experiences

Portions of the NDERF website, including the questionnaire, have been translated into 23 different languages. Over 500 near-death experiences in non- English languages have been shared with NDERF over the years. Dozens of volunteers have translated the non- English NDEs into English. Both the non-English and English translated versions of the NDEs are posted on the NDERF website. Over 60,000 people currently visit the NDERF website each month. Many website visitors are bilingual and this help assure that the NDEs are accurately translated.

My investigation of NDEs from around the world that have been translated into English shows that their content is strikingly similar. If near-death experiences were considerably influenced by pre-existing religious and cultural beliefs, it would be expected that there would be significant differences in the content of NDEs from different cultures around the world. However, in my review of over 500 NDEs from dozens of countries around the world I found impressive similarities in the content of these NDEs.

I investigated 19 non-Western NDEs, where a "non- Western country" was defined as areas of the world that are predominantly not of Jewish or Christian heritage. These 19 non-Western NDEs were compared to a group of NDEs shared in English from Western countries that were predominantly English speaking. This investigation concluded:

"All near-death experience elements appearing in Western NDEs are present in non-Western NDEs. There are many non-Western NDEs with narratives that are strikingly similar to the narratives of typical Western NDEs. At a minimum, it may be concluded that non- Western NDEs are much more similar to Western NDEs than dissimilar."

Two recent investigations of Muslim near-death experiences in non-Western countries have been reported. An investigation of 19 Iranian Muslim NDEs concluded:

"Our results suggest that Muslim NDEs may actually be quite common, as they are in the West, and may not be especially different in their key features from Western NDEs and therefore not heavily influenced by cultural variations, including prior religious or spiritual beliefs."

Another study of eight Muslim NDEs found:

"Although the documentation standard of the available cases is generally low, these accounts indicate that structure and contents of NDEs from many non-Western Muslim communities are largely similar to those reported in the Western NDE literature."

The lack of significant differences in the content of near-death experiences around the world, including NDEs from non-Western countries, suggests that NDE content is not substantially modified by pre-existing cultural influences. This finding is consistent with the previously discussed finding that children age five and under, who have received far less cultural influence than adults during their brief lives, have NDEs with content that is essentially the same as older children and adults. Other common forms of altered consciousness, such as dreams or hallucinations, are much more likely to be significantly influenced by prior cultural beliefs and life experiences. The lack of significant differences in the content of NDEs around the world is consistent with the concept that NDEs occur independently from physical brain function as currently understood.

Line of Evidence #9

Near-death experience after effects

Following near-death experiences significant changes in the lives of NDErs are commonly observed. The most recent version of the NDERF survey asked NDErs, "My experience directly resulted in...:"

The responses of 278 NDErs to the question were

Large changes in my life	152	54.7 %
Moderate changes in my life	68	24.5 %
Slight changes in my life	28	10.1 %
No changes in my life	14	5.0 %
Unknown	16	5.8 %

Changes in beliefs and values following near-death experiences are often called aftereffects. Given that a life-threatening event without an NDE might result in life changes, some of the best evidence for NDE-specific aftereffects came from the largest prospective NDE study ever reported. This study, conducted by Pim van Lommel, MD, divided survivors of cardiac arrest into a group that had NDEs, and a group that did not. The aftereffects of both groups were assessed two and eight years after the cardiac arrests. The group of cardiac arrest survivors with NDEs were statistically more likely have a reduced fear of death, increased belief in life after death, interest in the meaning of life, acceptance of others, and were more loving and empathic. It may take years after NDEs for the aftereffects to become fully manifest. The aftereffects may be so substantial that NDErs may seem to be very different people to their loved ones and family. The consistency, intensity, and durability of NDE aftereffects is consistent with the NDErs' typical personal assessments that their experiences were very meaningful and significant. It is remarkable that NDEs often occur during only minutes of unconsciousness, yet commonly result in substantial and life-long transformations of beliefs and values.

CONCLUSION OF STUDY

Multiple lines of evidence point to the conclusion that near-death experiences are medically inexplicable and cannot be explained by known physical brain function. Many of the preceding lines of evidence would be remarkable if they were reported by a group of individuals during conscious experiences. However, NDErs are generally unconscious or clinically dead at the time of their experiences and should not have any lucid organized memories from their time of unconsciousness.

It is informative to consider how near-death experiencers themselves view the reality of their experiences. An NDERF survey of 1122 NDErs asked "How do you currently view the reality of your experience?", and received the following responses:

Experience was definitely real	962	95.6 %
Experience was probably real	40	4.0 %
Experience was probably not real	3	0.3 %
Experience was definitely not real	1	0.1 %

The great majority of more than 1,000 near-death experiencers believed that their experiences were definitely real. The 1,122 NDErs surveyed included many physicians, scientists, attorneys, and nurses. These findings suggest that, for the majority of us who have not personally experienced an NDE, we should be very cautious about labelling NDEs as "unreal." Given that such a high percentage of NDErs consider their experiences to be "definitely real," it would be reasonable to accept their assessment of the reality of their personal experience unless there is good evidence that their experiences were not real.

After over 35 years of scholarly investigation of near-death experience, the totality of what is observed in NDEs has not been adequately explained based on physical brain function. It is beyond the scope of this article to review the many proposed "explanations" of near-death experience. Over the years, there have been over 20 different "explanations" of NDE suggested that cover the gamut of physiological, psychological, and cultural causes. If any one or several of these "explanations" were widely accepted as plausible, then there would be no need for so many different "explanations" of NDE. Among those who believe that physical brain function must explain everything that is experienced in all NDEs, there is no consensus whatsoever about how physical brain function produces NDEs.

CONCLUSION

The combination of the preceding nine lines of evidence converges on the conclusion that near-death experiences are medically inexplicable. Any one or several of the nine lines of evidence would likely be reasonably convincing to many, but the combination of all of the presented nine lines of evidence provides powerful evidence that NDEs are, in a word, real.

Written by

Jeffrey Long, MD, is a radiation oncologist in Houma, Louisiana and a recognized world expert on near-death experiences. Dr. Long established the non-profit Near Death Experience Research Foundation and a website forum (www.nderf.org) for people to share their ND

In the name of Allah, the Gracious, the Merciful

Six Major Beliefs In Islam

The following six beliefs are those that are commonly held by Muslims, as laid out in the Quran and Hadith.

1. Belief in the Oneness of God: Muslims believe that God is the creator of all things, and that God is all-powerful and all-knowing. God has no offspring, no race, no gender, no body, and is unaffected by the characteristics of human life.

2. Belief in the Angels of God: Muslims believe in angels, unseen beings who worship God and carry out God's orders throughout the universe.

3. Belief in the Books of God: Muslims believe that God revealed holy books or scriptures to a number of God's messengers. These include the Quran (given to Muhammad), the Torah (given to Moses), the Gospel (given to Jesus), the Psalms (given to David), and the Scrolls (given to Abraham). Muslims believe that these earlier scriptures in their original form were divinely revealed, but that only the Quran remains as it was first revealed to the prophet Muhammad (peace be upon him).

4. Belief in the Prophets or Messengers of God: Muslims believe that God's guidance has been revealed to humankind through specially appointed messengers, or prophets, throughout history, beginning with the first man, Adam, who is considered the first prophet. Twenty-five of these prophets are mentioned by name in the Quran, including Noah, Abraham, Moses, and Jesus. Muslims believe that Muhammad (peace be upon him) is the last in this line of prophets, sent for all humankind with the message of Islam.

5. Belief in the Day of Judgment: Muslims believe that on the Day of Judgment, humans will be judged for their actions in this life; those who followed God's guidance will be rewarded with paradise; those who rejected God's guidance will be punished with hell.

6. Belief in the Divine Decree: This article of faith addresses the question of God's will. It can be expressed as the belief that everything is governed by divine decree, namely that whatever happens in one's life is preordained, and that believers should respond to the good or bad that befalls them with thankfulness or patience. This concept does not negate the concept of "free will;" since humans do not have prior knowledge of God's decree, they do have freedom of choice.

BELIEVE IN THE 'UNSEEN

... It is (Quran) a guidance for the righteous,

Who believe in the unseen... [Quran – Surah al-Baqarah (The Cow– 2:2]

TO BELIEVE IN THE 'UNSEEN' is a fundamental constituent of the Muslim faith as mentioned in the verse quoted above.

To begin with, let us point out that the lack of knowledge about things does not necessarily mean that they do not exist. They may exist, but lie hidden behind the veil of the unknown. Later, either through the course of human investigation or through the agency of Divine revelation, they emerge from the realm of the unseen to that of the seen.

The term 'unseen' in its wider application is employed to cover everything which is not directly visible or audible. Likewise it also covers all that is not directly accessible through other human sensory faculties. In this respect we may also define the unseen as a domain which covers all forms of existence which lie beyond the direct access of the five senses. The things which belong to this category do not remain permanently inaccessible. They are inaccessible only with reference to a given period in time.

Barrier or Veil

"Behind them lies the intervening (Barzakh) barrier (stretching) to the day of their resurrection" (Quran - 23:99-100) meaning this veil is only temporary in this Universe and man who was created in Jannah (heaven), naturally has the capacity to see the unseen world if that barrier wasn't present.

This barzakh (barrier or veil) has been removed for the Prophets so they can see the Jinn and Angels.

It's interesting that Allah says the barzakh (barrier/veil) stretches to the day of judgment and not across space, this reference to time rather than location has significance in physics, relating to relativity, time (time dilation), the nature of the barrier (Barzakh) or field between the seen and unseen world, and the nature of how Angels exist in that world.

"Have you seen him who takes his own lust (vain desires) as his ilah (god), and Allah (God) knowing (him as such), left him astray, and sealed his hearing and his heart, and put a cover on his sight. Who then will guide him after Allah (God)? Will you not then remember?

And they say, "There is not but our worldly life; we die and live, and nothing destroys us except time." And they have of that no knowledge; they are only assuming.

And when Our Clear Verses are recited to them, their argument is no other than that they say: "Bring back our (dead) fathers, if you are truthful!" (Quran - 45:23-25)

"We have stripped from thee the Veil that covered thee and thy (inner) vision, this day is iron" (50:22).

Now that covering Veil (on the inner eye) is that of the imagination and fantasy (he "who makes his own desires his deity", the punishment for this is, "upon whose sight He has placed a veil?"); and therefore the man who has been deluded (blinded in his inner sight) by his own fancies, his false beliefs, and his vain imaginations replies (on that day): "Our Lord! We have seen Thee and heard Thee! O send us back and we will do good. Verily now we have certainty in knowledge!"

If we understand the physical world and the unseen world are the same Universe and that human consciousness or our soul is a state of matter, it is created from matter, and made from the small quantum particles (subatomic particles) that exist in the universe like light (Light behaves as both particles and waves at the same time), It becomes easier to realize that our minds inner sight (soul) is looking into the quantum unseen world.

If we imagine a brick wall in our mind, we are literally moving and arranging these quantum particles to form that image in our mind, that image of the brick wall is real and made from real substances.

The Messenger of Allah (saws) said: 'The angels are created from light (the scholars said it is the same light we see in our mind that shapes the images of our imagination), just as the Jinn are created from smokeless fire (a fire that isn't fuelled by wood burning) and mankind is created from what you have been told about (from clay).' (Hadith – Sahih Muslim)

The Angels are created from the same light we see in our mind so it isn't too difficult to see how they are charged with being inspiration for man's guidance and the bearers of Allah's revelation, which the Prophets received through their inner perceptive faculties. It also shouldn't be too difficult to see how the Jinn, who are being tested on earth like mankind can similarly be a source of inspiration for Good or Evil and they influence man through his perceptive faculties whispering to him what they want him to do.

Throughout the body is the nervous system, it is literally the bodies electrical wiring and it is connected to the brain, heart and every other organ in the body, it is this quantum aspect of man's physiology that beings made from quantum particles (light) such as Angels and Jinn can interact with man through, this reality everyone on earth is subject to throughout his life just like the Laws of physics.

Our inner perceptive faculty that sees the unseen world is the heart, it was reported from Jabir ibn Abdullah that some angels came to the Prophet (peace be upon him) while he was sleeping. Some of them said, "He is sleeping." Others said, "His eyes are sleeping but his heart is awake." Then they said, "There is an example for this companion of yours." One of them said, "Then set forth an example for him." Some of them said, "He is sleeping." The others said, "His eyes are sleeping but his heart is awake." Then they said, "His example is that of a man who has built a house and then offered therein a banquet and sent an inviter (messenger) to invite the people. So whoever accepted the invitation of the inviter, entered the house and ate of the banquet, and whoever did not accept the invitation of the inviter, did not enter the house, nor did he eat of the banquet." Then the angels said, "Interpret this example to him so that he may understand it." Some of them said, "He is sleeping." The others said, "His eyes are sleeping but his heart is awake." And then they said, "The house stands for Paradise and the call maker is Muhammad; and whoever obeys Muhammad, obeys Allah; and whoever disobeys Muhammad, disobeys Allah. Muhammad separated the people (i.e., through his message, the good is distinguished from the bad, and the believers from the disbelievers)." (Hadith – Sahih Bukhari)

The heart is our normal perceptive faculty present in all mankind, which Allah guides us through or punishes through, "We have revealed to you as We revealed to Nuh (Noah) and the Prophets who came after him." (Quran - 4:162), we follow the emotions we feel there and they are according to how we sense matters, a study of the hearts nervous system and the neurons present there will show it is a mini brain, built to sense and remember emotions, the hearts role and importance above the brain can be gaged by the fact that in the foetus the heart develops long before the brain does to regulate the body.

Imam Suyuti said, "Whomever Allah desires to guide, He expands his breast to Islam (believe in God is one), by casting into his heart a light which it [the heart] expands for and accepts, and whomever He,

Allah (God), desires to send astray, He makes his breast narrow". (Quran- 6:125, Tafsir al Jalalayn). The heart produces the largest electromagnetic field in the body, in literal terms it produces a field of light that can be measured by scientist, this electromagnetic field is produced my almost all living creatures and it is how they sense the world around them. When two waves touch, as physics states, they can become coherent, or synchronies with each other, and a transfer of information occurs between them without hindrance, non-coherent waves, that haven't synchronized, transfer information less clearly.

"And whosoever believe in Allah, He guide his heart. And Allah is knower of all things." (Quran - 64:11)

"And obey not him whose heart we have made heedless of Our Remembrance, who follow his own lust." (Quran - 18:28)

The heart is the faculty that receives information through our senses, Lust muddles the senses so the person cannot perceive clearly through his faculties.

It was once said: O Sayyid (Imam)! A gnostic of high degree used to say, 'Being a dervish (an ascetic) is to correct the imagination.' In other words, nothing other than the Real (Haq) should remain in the heart (Otherwise the imagination will only see the lies and false beliefs the evil heart contains). In truth, he spoke well. O Sayyid! Since the veil is nothing but imagination, the veil must be lifted through imagination. Night and day you must dwell in imagining Oneness of God (Tawhid). (Shaykh Baqi's son, Khwaja Khurd)

Tawhid of the heart here means un-attaching the heart from this world, not having any feelings or emotions towards anything in it and only remembering Allah (God). This lesson Allah (God) has been teaching mankind from the earliest of revelations He sent to man, Allah said, "But those will prosper who purify themselves (their inner selfs). And glorify the name of their Lord in prayer. No, you prefer the life of this world; But the hereafter is better and more enduring (here Allah is encouraging people to renounce the world).

And this is in the books of the earliest revelations. The books of Abraham and Moses. [Quran - Surah Al-Ala (The Most High) 87:14-19]

What is meant by "this day is iron," (50:22) is that what was veiling our inner sight (soul), the veil on our soul, will be lifted on this day (Qiyamah/Day of Judgement) and our inner eye (soul), will from now on be focused and see straight, permanently seeing the unseen world and everything Allah created in it like Heaven, Hell, the Angels and Jinn.

So what man once thought was imagination, illusion and unreal he will see with his inner eye (soul) clearly in front of him and it will be tangible and real to his vision like this world is, it will be solid to his eye as Iron (Hadid). The unseen world, like the Angels, is made from subatomic particles (light), the particles are smaller than atoms all linked together to create something bigger, like invisible light, it too is invisible to us, but we will be able to see when Allah lifts the barzakh (barrier/veil) from our soul and our lower self won't be present to muddy the picture in our mind creating delusions in us, we will only see what is actually there.

After Allah lifts the veil from all of mankind's sight on the day of Judgment He says about man in the Quran, "His companion (the Angel which accompanied man throughout his life and was right next him) will say: "Here is (your record) ready with me" (Quran - 50:23).

The first thing man will see when the veil from his inner sight (soul) is removed is his recording Angel who he was blind to his entire life

"We detail Our signs for people who know" (Quran - 6:97), "On the earth are Signs for those with certainty in Faith"(Quran - 51:20), The word "sign" (ayat) appears more than 351 times in the Qur'an instructing people to read the various kinds of signs that Allah has created for us.

The Prophet (Allah bless him and give him peace) said: "We, the Community of Prophets (Noah, Lot, Abraham, Joseph, David, Moses, John the Baptist, Jesus) are the people most severely tried, then others according to the perfection of their faith."

ANGELS

Most Muslims believe that angels or malaikah were created before humans with the purpose of following the orders of Allah and communicating with humans.

THE NATURE OF ANGELS

According to Islamic belief, the angels constantly praise God:

"They exalt Him night and day and do not slacken" (Quran - 21:20)

- They are part of God's creation – they had a beginning and they will exist until the end of time
- They are made of pure light
- They have wings, sometimes in pairs of two, three or four.
- They are extremely beautiful. With the exception of the Angel of Death.
- They are pure and always obey and serve Allah (God)
- They have no free will, or free will that is very restricted, as they must serve God faithfully as his messenger
- Angels can be of different size, status or merit.
- They can take on different forms.
- They cannot be described as male or female, as such an attribute is not assigned them.
- The number of Angels is unknown to anyone but Allah the All-Mighty.
- They can take on the form of humans
- The angels do not eat.

THE ROLE OF ANGELS

Angels have many and varied responsibilities assigned to them by the Creator. Some of the tasks we know Angels preside over are:

- To blow life into the foetus
- They act as messengers to the Prophets.
- They take care of people.
- They record everything a person does, and this information is used on the Day of Judgement.
- Izrail, the Angel of Death, takes people's souls when they die.
- They question people in the grave,
- They welcome People into Paradise and also supervise the pits of Hell.
- Blowing the Trumpet, which will be blown by Israfil (an angel) at the onset of the Hour (the Day of Judgement)
- Directing rain wherever Allah wishes. This is Mikail, upon whom be peace. He has helpers, who do what he tells them, by the command of his Lord; they direct the winds and clouds, as Allah (God) wills.

GUARDIAN ANGELS

"(Remember!) That the two receivers (recording angels) receive (each human being after he or she has attained the age of puberty), one sitting on the right and one on the left (to note his or her actions). Not a word does he (or she) utter, but there is a watcher by him ready (to record it)."— (Surah Qaf 50:17-18)

For each (person), there are angels in succession, before and behind him. They guard him by the Command of Allah. Verily! Allah will not change the good condition of a people as long as they do not change their state of goodness themselves (by committing sins and by being ungrateful and disobedient to Allah). But when Allah wills a people's punishment, there can be no turning back of it, and they will find besides Him no protector. [Surah Ar-Rad (The Thunder) - 13:11]

This verse emphasizes an important part of a guardian angel's job description: protecting people from danger. The Prophet (peace be upon him) said,

"Angels take turns around you, some at night and some by day, and all of them assemble together at the time of the Fajr (before sunrise) and 'Asr prayers (before sunset). Then those who have stayed with you throughout the night, ascend to Allah, who asks them, though he knows the answer better than they about you, 'How have you left my servants?' They reply, 'As we have found them praying, we have left them praying.'"— (Hadith - Sahih al-Bukhari Hadith 10:530)

ANGELS OBEYING ALLAH'S WILL

Muslims only ask Allah for help and only worship Him [Qur'an - Surat Al-Fatiha (The Opener) -1:5].

Human beings and jinn are the only creations of Allah who have a free will.

Everyone and everything else only does what Allah permits them to do.

Angels do not have free will. They obey Allah's commands without hesitation.

In other words, while the angels are protecting a person, it is by the will and permission of Allah.

If a calamity is to befall a person, the angels withdraw by the command of Allah. In other words the angels only follow the commands of Allah.

They, (angels) disobey not, the Commands they receive from God, but do that which they are commanded. [Quran - Surah At-Tahrim (The Prohibtiion) - 66:6]

ANGELS MENTION IN QURAN

Those whose lives the angels take while they are doing wrong to themselves (by disbelief and by associating partners in worship with Allah (God) and by committing all kinds of crimes and evil deeds)." Then, they will make (false) submission (saying): "We used not to do any evil." (The angels will reply): "Yes! Truly, Allah is All-Knower of what you used to do." [Surah An-Nahl (The Bee) 16:28]

"Honourable angels, recording ˹everything˺." [Surah Al-Infitar (The Cleaving) 82:11]

By those ˹angels˺ lined up in ranks,

By those (angels) who drive the clouds in a good way. By those (angels) who bring the Book and the Quran from Allah to mankind,

Verily your Ilah (God) is indeed One (i.e. Allah); [Surah AS-Saffat (Those who set the Ranks)-37:1-4]

That (this) is indeed an honourable recital (the Noble Quran).

In a Book well-guarded (with Allah in the heaven i.e. Al-Lauh Al-Mahfuz).

Which (that Book with Allah) none can touch but the purified (i.e. the angels). [Surah Al-Waqiah (The Inevitable)-56:77-79]

When the angels seize the souls of those who have wronged themselves—scolding them, "What do you think you were doing?" they will reply, "We were oppressed in the land." The angels will respond, "Was Allah's earth not spacious enough for you to emigrate?" It is they who will have Hell as their home—what an evil destination! [Surah An-Nisa (The Women)-4:97]

And he would never ask you to take angels and prophets as lords. Would he ask you to disbelieve after you have submitted? [Surah al-Imran (Family of Imran)-3:80]

And to Allah ˹alone˺ bows down ˹in submission˺ whatever is in the heavens and whatever is on the earth of living creatures, as do the angels—who are not too proud ˹to do so˺. [Surah An-Nahl (The Bee) -16:49]

And they say: "The Most Beneficent (Allah) has begotten a son (or children)." Glory to Him! They [those whom they call children of Allah i.e. the angels, 'Iesa (Jesus) son of Maryam (Mary), 'Uzair (Ezra), etc.], are but honoured slaves. [Surah Al-Anbya (The Prophets) -21:26]

˹The angels announced,˺ "O Zachariah! Indeed, We give you the good news of ˹the birth of˺ a son, whose name will be John—a name We have not given to anyone before." [Surah Maryam (Mary) - 19:7]

˹Allah will say to the angels,˺ "Gather ˹all˺ the wrongdoers along with their peers, and whatever they used to worship [Surah Aṣ-Ṣaffat (Those who set the Ranks) -37:22]

And the angels glorify the praises of their Lord, and seek forgiveness for those on earth. Surely Allah alone is the All-Forgiving, Most Merciful. [Surah Ash-Shuraa (The Consultation) - 42:5]

They ˹all˺ believe in Allah, His angels, His Books, and His messengers. ˹They proclaim,˺ "We make no distinction between any of His messengers." And they say, "We hear and obey. ˹We seek˺ Your forgiveness, our Lord! And to You ˹alone˺ is the final return." [Surah Al-Baqarah (The Cow) - 2:285]

It is not given to any human being that Allah should speak to him unless (it be) by Inspiration, or from behind a veil, or (that) He sends a Messenger to reveal what He wills by His Leave. Verily, He is Most High, Most Wise. [Surah Ash-Shuraa (The Consultation) 42:51]

Who is more unjust than one who invents a lie against Allah or rejects His Ayat (proofs, evidences, verses, lessons, signs, revelations, etc.)? For such their appointed portion (good things of this worldly life and their period of stay therein) will reach them from the Book (of Decrees) until, when Our Messengers (the angel of death and his assistants) come to them to take their souls, they (the angels) will say:

"Where are those whom you used to invoke and worship besides Allah," they will reply, "They have vanished and deserted us." And they will bear witness against themselves, that they were disbelievers. [Surat Al-Araf (The Heights) -7:37]

And who is more unjust than one who invents a lie about Allah (God) or says, "It has been inspired to me," while nothing has been inspired to him, and one who says, "I will reveal [something] like what Allah (God) revealed." And if you could but see when the wrongdoers are in the overwhelming pangs of death while the angels extend their hands, [saying], "Discharge your souls! Today you will be awarded the punishment of [extreme] humiliation for what you used to say against Allah (God) other than the truth and [that] you were, toward His verses, being arrogant." [Surah Al-Anam (The Cattle) - 6:93]

And those who kept their duty to their Lord will be led to Paradise in groups, till, when they reach it, its gates will be opened and its keepers will say: Salamun 'alaikum (peace be upon you!). You have done well, so enter here, to abide therein. [39:73]

For those who say. 'Our Lord is Allah,' and then take the straight path towards Him, the angels come down to them and say, 'Have no fear or grief, but rejoice in the good news of Paradise which you have been promised. We are your allies in this world and the world to come, where you will have everything you desire and ask for as a welcoming gift from the Most Forgiving, Most Merciful.' [Surat Fussilat (Explained in Detail) - 41:30-32]

FACTS ABOUT ANGELS IN ISLAM

1. **How many angels do you have specifically assigned to you?**

Every one of us has 4 angels assigned to us! 2 that protect us (1 in front and 1 behind), and 2 that record us (1 on each side of us)

2. **Do angels have wings?**

"Praise be to God, Creator of the heavens and earth, who made angels messengers with two, three, four [pairs of] wings. He adds to creation as He will: God has power over everything." [Quran - Surah Faṭir (Originator) - 35:1]

3. Can angels take on a human-like form?

Then We sent to her [Maryam/Mary] Our angel, and he appeared before her as a man in all respects," [Quran - Surah Maryam (Mary) - 19:17]

4. Are angels capable of disobeying Allah?

"Believers, guard yourselves and your families against a Fire fuelled by people and stones, over which stand angels, stern and strong; angels who never disobey God's commands to them, but do as they are ordered:" [Quran - Surah At-Tahrim (The Prohibtiion) - 66:6]

5. What are angels made from?

The Prophet (S) said:

"The angels were created from light, the jinn were created from fire, and Adam was created from (clay) that which has been described to you" [Hadith - Sahih Muslim, 5314]

6. What are the names of the angels that watch over heaven and hell?

Ridwan (Heaven) and Malik (Hell)

"They will cry, 'Malik, if only your Lord would finish us off,' but he will answer, 'No! You are here to stay.'" [Quran - Surah Az-Zukhruf (The Ornaments of Gold) -43:77]

7. How many angels will question us in our graves?

Munkar and Nakir [Arabic: منكر ونكير) (English translation: "The Denied and The Denier")] are the two angels assigned to question people in their graves about their faith.

8. **Does the angel recording our bad deeds to the left of us write them down into our Record immediately?**

It is reported that the Prophet (S) said:

"Truly the Angel on the left [of a person] withholds from recording the sinful deed committed by the Muslim servant who sinned for a period six 'hours'. If the servant regrets committing the sin and asks Allah for forgiveness, the Angel does not write down his sin. Otherwise, the angel records it as one bad deed." [Hadith - at-Tabarani, al-Mu`jam al-Kabir]

9. **Do angels eat and drink?**

No, angels do not eat or drink.

"Then he (Abraham) turned to his household, so brought out a roasted calf [as the property of Ibrahim (Abraham) was mainly cows]. And placed it before them (angels in human form), (saying): "Will you not eat?" Then he conceived a fear of them (when they ate not). They said: "Fear not." And they gave him glad tidings of an intelligent son, having knowledge (about Allah and His religion of True Monotheism)." [Quran - Surat Adh-Dhariyat (The Winnowing Winds) - 51:26-28]

SATAN

HISTORY OF SATAN (IBLIS)

Satan was created from smokeless fire. Though he was not an angel, he was present amongst them in Heaven due to his obedience to Allah (God). When Allah created Prophet Adam (peace be upon him), He commanded those in Heaven to prostrate before Adam, but Satan refused out of pride and arrogance, saying, "I am better than him [Adam], You created me from fire, and created him from clay." [Quran – Surah Al-Araf (The Heights) 7:12]

Allah cursed Satan and banished him from Heaven. Satan requested an opportunity to mislead mankind, and Allah granted this request.

"[Satan] said, 'Because You have put me in error, I will surely sit in wait for them [mankind] on Your straight path. Then I will come to them from before them and from behind them and on their right and on their left, and You will not find most of them grateful [to You].'" [Quran – Surah Al-Araf (The Heights) 7:16-17]

GRADUAL DECEPTION

Prophet Muhammad (peace be upon him) explained to us how idol worship originated, which highlights the gradual and patient approach of Satan. After a group of righteous people died, Satan inspired those around them to erect statues in their honour and as reminder of their righteousness. When that generation passed away and the people had forgotten why the statues were erected, Satan deceived them into believing that their forefathers used to worship them, and that through them, the rains were brought forth. People then began worshipping these statues.

This gradual deception is used in many ways. For example, Satan tricks people into committing forbidden sexual acts: it begins with a look, which leads to a thought, then a smile, then a seemingly innocent conversation, then seclusion and eventually, the sin itself.

BEAUTIFYING EVIL DEEDS

"...And Satan made attractive to them that which they were doing." [Quran - Surah Al-Anam (The Cattle) 6:43]

Satan presents sins to people in a favourable light, such as how he deceived Adam and Eve into eating from the tree.

Satan whispered to Adam, saying, "'O Adam! Shall I lead you to the Tree of Eternity and to a kingdom that will never waste away?' " (Quran - Surah Taha - 20:120)

"'Your Lord did not forbid you this tree except that you become angels or become of the immortal... Indeed, I am (Satan) to you from among the sincere advisors.' So he made them fall, through deception. And when they tasted of the tree... their Lord called to them, 'Did I not forbid you from that tree and tell you that Satan is to you a clear enemy?' " [Quran – Surah Al-Araf (The Heights) 7:20-22]

✓ Arousing Desires

"Satan promises them and arouses desire in them. But Satan does not promise them except delusion." (Quran 4:120)

Every human has desires and temptations. Satan plays on this and convinces man to indulge in instant gratification without considering the consequences. This inevitably leads to regret and humiliation, either in this life or on the Day of Judgement.

✓ The Traps of Satan

Disbelief in the Oneness of God

The foundation of Islam is the belief in the Oneness of God - having no partner, equal, son or rivals. Conversely, the greatest sin is to ascribe partners or equals with Allah.

Examples include:

Directing worship to other than God (e.g. prostrating or supplicating to other than God).

Delegating some of God's attributes to other objects or beings (e.g. idols/lucky charms).

Claiming that God has a son, mother or any other partner.

Thus, tempting mankind into disbelief is Satan's main focus. However, if Satan cannot mislead people to commit clear acts of disbelief, he resorts to more subtle means, such as the belief in superstitions, good luck charms, astrology and fortune telling. Such beliefs contradict the fact that Allah alone has power and knowledge over all things, and is the Only One Who can bring benefit or harm.

WHAT IS SOUL?

Self-knowledge is vital to the spiritual development of every Muslim believer (believe in God is one). One must know the make-up of his or her psyche in order to optimally improve it. Islam provides us with a blueprint of the human soul for this very purpose.

The psyche (inner-self) of an individual is composed of four parts: the heart (qalb), the spirit (ruh), the self or ego (nafs), and the mind ('aql). Each part reflects a different aspect of the psyche, although they interact with each other in ways that overlap.

The first term "heart" can refer to the corporeal heart, the physical organ within the chest that pumps blood throughout the body. It can also refer to the ethereal heart, the inner-most consciousness that is the essence of the human being.

Al-Ghazali writes:

The second meaning of heart is a subtle, heavenly, and spiritual substance it has, which is related to the physical heart. This subtle substance is the true essence of the human being. It is the conscious, knowing, and perceiving part of the human being. It is addressed, punished, blamed, and accountable. (Source: Uluum al-Din 3/3)

The ethereal heart should be our most important concern, because no one will benefit on the Day of Judgment unless they bring a pure heart with them.

Allah said:

يَوْمَ لَا يَنْفَعُ مَالٌ وَلَا بَنُونَ إِلَّا مَنْ أَتَى اللَّهَ بِقَلْبٍ سَلِيمٍ

A Day in which wealth and children will not benefit, except one who comes to Allah with a pure heart. [Quran - Surah al-Shu'ara (The Poets) - 26:88-89]

Both the physical and ethereal hearts are essential for the health of the human being. If the physical heart is damaged or malfunctioning, it can quickly lead to sudden death. If the ethereal heart is corrupted by spiritual diseases, it will lead to a type of spiritual death and damnation in the Hereafter.

Al-Nu'man ibn Bashir reported: The Messenger of Allah, peace and blessings be upon him, said:

Verily, in the body is a piece of flesh which, if sound, the entire body is sound, and if corrupt, the entire body is corrupt. Truly, it is the heart. (Hadith - Sahih al-Bukhari - 52)

The second term "spirit" can refer to the life-force that permeates and animates the body. When the spirit is removed, the body will die. It can also refer to the higher-self, the capacity of a human being to receive divine inspiration (ilham) and guidance from Allah.

Allah said:

وَيَسْأَلُونَكَ عَنِ الرُّوحِ ۖ قُلِ الرُّوحُ مِنْ أَمْرِ رَبِّي وَمَا أُوتِيتُم مِّنَ الْعِلْمِ إِلَّا قَلِيلًا

They ask you about the spirit. Say: The spirit is among the affairs of my Lord, you have been given little knowledge of it. [Quran - Surat al-Isra (The Night Journey) - 17:85]

The spirit has a lordly and heavenly quality (rabbani), meaning it is the aspect of the psyche that reflects the attributes of the Creator. Allah blew His created spirit into human beings, resulting in their ability to see, to hear, and to perceive with their hearts.

Allah said:

ثُمَّ سَوَّاهُ وَنَفَخَ فِيهِ مِن رُّوحِهِ ۖ وَجَعَلَ لَكُمُ السَّمْعَ وَالْأَبْصَارَ وَالْأَفْئِدَةَ ۚ قَلِيلًا مَّا تَشْكُرُونَ

Then, He fashioned him and blew into him from His spirit. He made for you hearing, seeing, and hearts, yet little are you grateful. [Quran - Surah al-Sajdah (The Prostration) - 32:8]

Al-Baydawi commented on this verse, writing:

It adds nobility to himself and indicates that humanity is a wondrous creation, that his prestige is appropriate enough to enter the presence of the Lord. For this reason, it is said: Whoever knows himself, knows his Lord. (Source: Tafsir al-Baydawi 32:8)

The third term "self" can refer to a person's identity or the composite whole of their psyche. This is how the term is commonly used in ordinary language. As a specific term, the self can refer to the lower-self, ego, or id, which is the receptacle of basic sensations, emotions, and instincts like fear, aggression, and carnal desire.

Allah said:

وَأَمَّا مَنْ خَافَ مَقَامَ رَبِّهِ وَنَهَى النَّفْسَ عَنِ الْهَوَىٰ فَإِنَّ الْجَنَّةَ هِيَ الْمَأْوَىٰ

As for him who feared to stand before his Lord and he restrained his ego from his whims, Paradise will be his refuge. [Quran - Surah al-Naziat (Those who drag forth) - 79:40]

For this reason, many scholars referred to the 'self' as an enemy against which we should wage spiritual war. The true jihad (war), in fact, is to fight in jihad (war) against the lower-self and its whims.

Fadalah ibn Ubayd reported: The Messenger of Allah, peace and blessings be upon him, said:

The one who strives in jihad (war) is he who strives against his ego. (Hadith - Sunan al-Tirmidhi 1621)

It is in this context that Sahl ibn Abdullah, may Allah have mercy on him, said:

If one knows the enemy, one knows his Lord. (Source: Hdilyat al-Awliya 10/201)

The fourth term "mind" likewise has various shades of meaning that overlap with the other terms. It is generally distinguished from the other terms as the intellectual capacity of human beings to reason, think, know, contemplate, reflect, and understand.

The mind is very important because it is the receptacle of conscious thought, where reflection takes place and ideas are contemplated and understood. It is considered to be one of the pillars of being human.

Umar ibn al-Khattab, may Allah be pleased with him, said:

The foundation of a man is his mind, his honor is in his religion, and his manhood is in his character. (Source: Adab al-Dunya wal-Din 1/17)

The mind influences the heart by the conscious thoughts we choose to entertain. We are not responsible and do not have control over automatic or involuntary thoughts, which arise from the lower-self or the whispering of Satan (devil). Rather, we are responsible and have control over the thoughts we deliberately engage. Gaining mastery over our conscious thoughts and changing negative thought-patterns is a psychological skill called cognitive restructuring, which can be cultivated through mindfulness practice.

All evil deeds are preceded by evil thoughts, and all harmful thoughts can cause physical and emotional distress, such as depression and anxiety. Good thoughts come from the higher-self, and bad thoughts comes from the lower-self or Satan. These thoughts can have a profound effect on the feelings we experience and the actions we undertake, so one must learn the mindfulness skill of shutting down bad trains of thought as they arise.

Ibn al-Qayyim writes:

For a thought turns into a suggestion, and a suggestion becomes an intention, and an intention strengthens until it becomes a determination, then it becomes an action, then it becomes a necessary description, a form established and grounded. In that case, it becomes impossible to expel them just as it is impossible to expel an enduring characteristic. (Source: al-Da wal-Dawa 1/158)

The Souls Form

According to Ibn al-Qayyim description of the "souls" form described and explained as follows:

"The spirit/soul is an entity which differs from the physical, tangible body. It is a higher type of luminous (or light-like) being, alive and moving, and it penetrates the limbs, circulating through them as water circulates throughout the petals of a rose, as oil circulates throughout the olive, and as fire circulates throughout the burning embers of coal."

Souls Are Like Conscripted Soldiers

Abu Huraira reported Allah's Messenger (ﷺ) Saying:

Souls are troops collected together and those who familiarised with each other (in the heaven from where these come) would have affinity, with one another (in the world) and those amongst them who opposed each other (in the Heaven) would also be divergent (in the world). (Hadith - Sahih Muslim Book 45, Hadith 204)

Two Deaths and Two Lives

In the Quran Allah has mentioned two deaths and two lives.

How can you disbelieve in Allah? Seeing that you were dead and He gave you life. Then He will give you death, then again will bring you to life (on the Day of Resurrection) and then unto Him you will return. [Quran - Al Baqarah (The Cow) - 2:28]

They will say: "Our Lord! You have made us to die twice (i.e. we were dead in the loins of our fathers and dead after our deaths in this world), and You have given us life twice (i.e. life when we were born and life when we are Resurrected)! Now we confess our sins, then is there any way to get out (of the Fire)?" [Quran – Surah Ghafir (The Forgiver) -40:11]

The first death is the state of the soul when it was first created. Allah creates first of all from the sperm, it turns into 'Alaqa' (leach like substance in the womb), then the 'Mugarah' (little piece of flesh), and when it is in the shape of a fetus (after 120 days), the soul is breathed into it. This is the moment when life begins. When the soul leaves the body (when death occurs), this is the second death and then Allah (swt) gives them a new form and this is the second life.

This life now is the most important one, because what we do in this life, determines what happens in the next.

A third of our life is spent in sleeping. While we are sleeping our souls leave our body.

It is Allah Who takes away the souls at the time of their death, and those that die not during their sleep. He keeps those (souls) for which He has ordained death and sends the rest for a term appointed. Verily, in this are signs for a people who think deeply. [Quran - Az-Zumar (The Troops) - 39:42]

THE MEETINGS OF SOULS

Souls of the Dead Meeting with Each Other

The souls of the dead may be divided into the following two categories:

1. Favored souls (i.e. those of pious believers)

2. Punished souls (i.e. those of the sinful believers and disbeliever's)

The souls of the second group are confined to places of punishment and are too preoccupied with the torments of the grave to be able to meet or visit with each other. However, the blessed and favored souls of the pious believers are free to roam and meet. They may visit and discuss with each other their previous existence on earth. In the barzakh (after death) every soul will be with companions of like nature. (refer: Ibn al-Qayyim's Kitab ar-Ruh page 28)

The following Hadith is a direct reference and clear proof that, in general, the souls of pious believers are able to meet and converse with each other.

Souls of The Dead Meeting with Souls of The Sleeping

Since the souls of the living (which are sleeping) and the souls of the dead can roam in the spiritual world - for they are not tied to their earthly bodies - it is certainly possible that they meet and converse. This deduction is confirmed by the majority of dependable Quranic commentators, foremost among them; Imam Ibn Jareer at-Tabari and Ibn Katheer.

Allah says in the Qur'an:

"Allah takes the souls at the time of death and (the souls) of those that do not die during their sleep. He retains those souls for which He has ordained death, whereas he releases the rest for an appointed term." [Quran - Az-Zumar (The Troops) -39:42]

Ibn al-Qayyim mentions two viewpoints regarding the tafseer on this verse. The first view is there are two points in time at which Allah takes souls: death and during sleep. Death may occur during sleeping or at other times. The soul taken at death is "retained" soul referred to in this verse. The "released" soul is that which is taken during sleep and is returned to its respective body upon awakening.

The second position in regard to this verse is that both the "retained" soul and the "released" one are taken during sleep. Then those who have completed their specified period of life are retained, while those who have not completed their time are returned to their bodies. This view suggests that the verse refers to only souls that die in their sleep and the souls which are returned to their respective bodies upon awakening, and does not mention the "retained" souls that die at times other than during sleep.

When I was researching this topic: I found it very hard to get information from the Qur'an and Authentic Sunnah of the Prophet (saws)

I think an appropriate way to finish is to re-quote the ayah from the beginning of this paper:

"And they ask you (O Muhammad) concerning the Ruh (the spirit): Say: "The Ruh (the spirit): its knowledge is with my Lord, And of knowledge, you (mankind) have been given but a little." [Quran - Al-Isra (The Night Journey) -17:85]

THE SOUL AFTER DEATH

Allāh's Messenger (peace be upon him) furnished us with more detail concerning what happens to the soul at the time of death:

When the believing servant is at the point of leaving this world and is about to enter the next, angels of mercy descend from the heaven, their faces white and radiant like the sun. With two of them is a shroud from the fabric of Paradise made of the softest, finest white silk, and perfume from the fragrance of Paradise. These two angels keep their distance, and the others sit around him stretching back as far as the eye can see. Then the Angel of Death arrives, having the best of forms and most fragrant of scents, and sits by his head saying, 'O pure soul, at peace and rest depart to Allāh's forgiveness and good pleasure.' The angels will also say words of encouragement, 'O pure soul which was in a pure body, leave the body in a praiseworthy state pleased and well-pleasing, and have glad tidings of Allāh's rest and ease. Go to a Lord who is not angry.' They will repeat this until the soul leaves the body, and on hearing these words, the soul will leave, exiting the body as easily as water drops fall from the spout of a water skin, or sweat leaves the body. The eyes follow the soul as it leaves and the Angel of Death will receive it.

No sooner does he take it, within the blink of an eye, the two angels rush forward and take it from his hand, place it in the shroud and perfume it, and all the angels pass it amongst themselves, taking in the ethereal scent.

When the soul has left the body, all the angels between the heavens and the earth, and all the angels in the heaven send ṣalāh (salutation) on him. They say, 'A pure soul has come from the earth, may Allāh send his ṣalāh (salutation) upon you and upon the body in which you lived.' The gates of the heavens open for him and the guardians of every gate implore Allāh that his soul ascends in their direction.

From the soul emanates the most exquisite scent of musk that ever existed on earth and two angels ascend with it. As they pass by gatherings of angels, they are asked, 'What is this good soul?' They reply, 'He is so-and-so, the son of so-and-so,' using the best names with which he had been addressed in this life. They say, 'Welcome to this pure soul that used to be in a pure body.' When they reach the lowest heaven, they request admission and the gates open for them and the angels there exclaim, 'What a beautiful scent you have brought from the earth!' The most select angels of each heaven will escort him to the next one until he reaches the seventh heaven, finally standing before Allāh by the Throne, and all the while the angels will keep supplicating for him. Allāh then says, "Write my servants record in illiyyūn,"

وَمَا أَدْرَاكَ مَا عِلِّيُّونَ ﴿١٩﴾ كِتَابٌ مَّرْقُومٌ ﴿٢٠﴾ يَشْهَدُهُ الْمُقَرَّبُونَ

What will explain to you what ʿilliyyūn is? A clearly written record witnessed by those brought near. [Quran – Surah al-Muṭaffifīn (The Defrauding) – 83:19-21]

His records are inscribed in ʿilliyyūn and Allāh will say to Angels Brought Close, "Bear witness that I have forgiven the person who has deeds such as these!" The angels are then told, 'Take him back to the earth because I promised them that from it I created them, into it shall I send them, and from it resurrect them once again. He is then returned to the earth and his soul returned to his body and at that point, he will hear the patter of his companion's shoes as they walk away from his grave.

When a disbelieving servant is at the point of leaving this world and about to enter the next, angels of punishment, severe and stern, with dark faces descend to him from the heavens. With them are coarse garments of the Fire and they sit around him, stretching back as far as the eye can see. The Angel of Death arrives and sits by his head, saying, 'Vile soul, depart to Allāh's wrath and anger.' The angels will say, 'Vile soul which lived in a vile body, leave the body in a blameworthy state, displeased and with displeasure on you. Go to Allāh's punishment! Have tidings of scalding water and foul pus, and other such punishments! They will keep repeating this until it leaves the body but on hearing this, terrified, the soul clings to the body, refusing to leave. The Angel of Death will extract it by force, like a skewer is pulled from wet wool causing the veins and nerves to burst. It will come out from the side of his mouth (filthy and noisy) like a donkey does when its soul departs.

No sooner does he take it, within the blink of an eye, the other angels take it from his hand and put it in that course fabric, and from it emanates the most repugnant odour of a decaying corpse that ever existed on the earth.

Every angel between the heavens and the earth, and every angel in the heavens, curses him. They said, 'A vile soul has come from the earth!' The gates of the heaven are barred to him, and the guardians of every gate implore Allāh that this soul not ascend in their direction.

The angels then ascend with it. As they pass by gatherings of angels, they are asked, "What is this vile soul?" They respond, 'He is so-and-so, son of so-and-so,' using the worst names with which he was called in this life. When they reach the lowest heaven, they request admission but the gates are not opened for him, and the angels say, 'What a vile odour! There is no welcome for a filthy soul living in a filthy body here! Return disgraced and humiliated, the door will not be opened for you!'

لَا تُفَتَّحُ لَهُمْ أَبْوَابُ السَّمَاءِ وَلَا يَدْخُلُونَ الْجَنَّةَ حَتَّىٰ يَلِجَ الْجَمَلُ فِي سَمِّ الْخِيَاطِ

The gates of heaven will not be open to them and they will not enter Paradise until a camel passes through the eye of a needle. [Quran - al-Araf (The Heights) - 7:40]

Allah will then say, "Write his record in Sijjin in the lowest earth," and they are told, 'Take him back to the earth because I promised them that from it I created them, into it I will send them, and from it resurrect them once again.' His soul is then cast down from the heavens without regard and it falls back into his body,

وَمَن يُشْرِكْ بِاللَّهِ فَكَأَنَّمَا خَرَّ مِنَ السَّمَاءِ فَتَخْطَفُهُ الطَّيْرُ أَوْ تَهْوِي بِهِ الرِّيحُ فِي مَكَانٍ سَحِيقٍ

Whoever associates partners with Allāh is like someone who has been hurled down from the skies and snatched up by birds or flung to a distant place by the wind. [Quran – Surah al-Ḥajj (The Pilgrimage) - 22:31]

And at that point, he will hear the patter of his companion's shoes as they walk away from his grave.

AFTERLIFE

Akhirah is the term for life after death. Muslims believe that no soul may die except with God's permission at a predestined time,

"Nor can a soul die except by Allah's leave. The term being fixed as by writing." [Quran - Surah al-Imran (Family of Imran) - 3:145]

Muslims believe in the concept of Paradise (Jannah), which is where people go if they have lived a good life. Muslims also believe in Hell (Jahannam), which is where people go if they have lived a bad life or have committed shirk [worship of anyone or anything besides Allah (God)].

Before Muslims go to Jannah or Jahannam, they go to Barzakh. This is where souls wait before the Day of Judgement. It is also a place that divides the living from the dead.

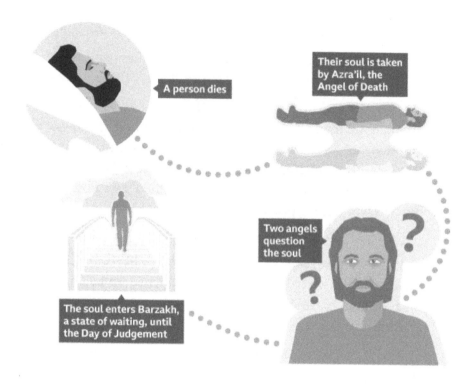

A person dies

Their soul is taken by Azra'il, the Angel of Death

Two angels question the soul

The soul enters Barzakh, a state of waiting, until the Day of Judgement

DAY OF JUDGEMENT

Yawm ad-Din is the Day of Judgement, when Allah will decide how people will spend their afterlife.

Most Muslims believe they have free will to make their own choices. They also believe that they will be judged by God for those choices. They recognise that humans are still responsible for their actions.

When God's purpose for the universe has been fulfilled, the world will be destroyed.

When the world ends, Israfil will sound a trumpet and there will be a resurrection. All the dead bodies will be raised and will gather on the plain of Arafat for the final judgement.

When the bodies are raised from the dead, they will be naked so that nothing can be hidden. They will also be given their own 'book of deeds'. They will take it in turns to read aloud from their book so that nothing can be hidden.

Those who are handed their deeds in their right hand will go to Heaven, and those who are handed them in their left hand will go to Hell.

The idea of a Day of Judgement encourages Muslims to live their lives in a good way. They try to pass the test of life and take responsibility for their actions, whether good or bad.

Muslims can also ask for forgiveness and they recognise that intention is important. For example, if a person carries out an action because they intend the result to be good but the outcome is unexpectedly bad, a good deed will still have been done as the intention was good. The Quran says:

"But when there comes the Deafening Blast - that Day a man will flee from his brother, and his mother and his father, and his wife and his children. For each one of them that Day will have enough preoccupations of his own. Some faces, that Day, will be bright – laughing, rejoicing at good news. And other faces, that Day, will have upon them dust. Blackness will cover them. Those are the disbelievers, the wicked ones." (Quran 80: 33-42)

When the record of every one's deeds is placed before him, you will see the criminals terrified from what the record contains. They will say, "Woe to us! What kind of record is this that has missed nothing small or great?" They will find whatever they have done right before their very eyes. Your Lord is not unjust to any one. (Quran 18:49)

And fear a Day when you will be returned to Allah (God). Then every soul will be compensated for what it earned, and they will not be treated unjustly. (Quran 2:281).

Heaven

In Islam, Heaven or Paradise is known as Jannah. In the Quran, the language used to describe Heaven is very descriptive. It is regarded as a place of:

- bliss
- reward
- pleasure for eternity

Muslims believe that people will be reunited with their families in Jannah, where they will enjoy the pleasures of being in a beautiful garden. The Quran says:

"And give good tidings to those who believe and do righteous deeds that they will have gardens [in Paradise] beneath which rivers flow. Whenever they are provided with a provision of fruit therefrom, they will say, 'This is what we were provided with before.' And it is given to them in likeness. And they will have therein purified spouses, and they will abide therein eternally." (Q. 2:25)

"Their Lord gives them good tidings of mercy from Him and approval and of gardens for them wherein is enduring pleasure. [They will be] abiding therein forever. Indeed, Allah has with Him a great reward." (Q. 9:21-22)

"Those will have gardens of perpetual residence; beneath them rivers will flow. They will be adorned therein with bracelets of gold and will wear green garments of fine silk and brocade, reclining therein on adorned couches. Excellent is the reward, and good is the resting place." (Q. 18:31)

"...the chosen servants of Allah. Those will have a provision determined—fruits; and they will be honored in gardens of pleasure on thrones facing one another. There will be circulated among them a cup from a flowing spring, white and delicious to the drinkers; no bad effect is there in it, nor from it will they be intoxicated." (Q. 37:40-47)

"[Other] faces, that Day, will show pleasure. With their effort [they are] satisfied. In an elevated garden, wherein they will hear no unsuitable speech. Within it is a flowing spring. Within it are couches raised high and cups put in place and cushions lined up and carpets spread around." (Q. 88:8-16)

HELL

Muslims often refer to Hell as Jahannam. It is a place of:

- eternal punishment
- mental torment
- physical torment

Descriptions of Hell detail some of the physical punishments that people will suffer for eternity. Hell is often described as a place of fire for those who have lived an evil life and not believed in Allah (God). The Quran says:

But those who reject Our signs are the companions of the left hand – on them will be fire vaulted over. (Quran 90:19-20)

"But he whose balance (of good deeds) is found to be light, will have his home in a (bottomless) Pit. And what will explain to you what this is? A Fire blazing fiercely!" (Quran - 101:8-11).

The unbelievers will be led to Hell in crowds until, when they arrive there, its gates will be opened (Quran 39: 71)

And verily, Hell is the promised abode for them all. It has seven gates: to each of those gates is a specific class of sinners assigned. (Quran 15: 43-44)

To them will be said, 'Enter you the gates of Hell to dwell therein. And how evil is this abode of the arrogant.' (Quran 39: 72)

Is Paradise better as an abode or the tree of zaqūm? Indeed, We have made it a torment for the wrongdoers. Indeed, it is a tree issuing from the bottom of the Hellfire, its emerging fruit as if it was heads of the devils. And, indeed, they will eat from it and fill with it their bellies. Then, indeed, they will have after it a mixture of scalding water. Then, indeed, their return will be to the Hellfire. (Quran 37:62-68)

"...Those who deny (their Lord), for them will be cut out a garment of Fire. Over their heads will be poured out boiling water. With it will be scalded what is within their bodies, as well as (their) skins. In addition there will be maces of iron (to punish) them. Every time they wish to get away therefrom, from anguish, they will be forced back, and (it will be said), "Taste the Penalty of Burning!" (Quran - 22:19-22).

"And those who followed would say: 'If only We had one more chance...' Thus will Allah show them (the fruits of) their deeds as (nothing but) regrets. Nor will there be a way for them out of the Fire" (Quran - 2:167)

"As to those who reject Faith: if they had everything on earth, and twice repeated, to give as ransom for the penalty of the Day of Judgment, it would never be accepted of them. Theirs would be a grievous penalty. Their wish will be to get out of the Fire, but never will they get out. Their penalty will be one that endures" (Quran - 5:36-37).

"Those who reject Faith, and die rejecting,- on them is Allah's curse, and the curse of angels, and of all mankind. They will abide therein: Their penalty will not be lightened, nor will they receive respite" (Quran - 2:161-162)

THE PURPOSE OF LIFE ACCORDING TO ISLAM

What is the purpose of life? The Holy Quran, believed by Muslims to be the direct word of God to humanity, encourages us to ask this question:

"Did you then think that We created you in vain, and that you would not be returned to Us?" (Holy Quran 23:115).

God associates the value of justice with the belief in a purpose to life:

"And We have not created the heaven and earth and what is between them in vain. That is the opinion of those who disbelieve. And woe to such disbelievers, because of the Fire. Shall we treat those who believe and do good deeds as those who spread corruption on the earth? Or shall we treat the pious as sinners?"(Holy Quran 38:27-8)

BELIEF AND GOOD DEEDS

The Holy Quran teaches that the purpose of life is to worship our Creator by believing in Him and by doing good deeds:

"And I created not the jinn and mankind except that they should worship Me (alone)." (Holy Quran 51:56)

"[He] Who has created life and death so that He may try you which of you are best in deeds…" (Holy Quran 67:2)

Believing in God and doing good deeds benefits our souls. The Quran teaches that the truly successful people are those who purify their souls:

"By the soul, and the proportion and the order given to it; and its enlightenment as to its wrong or right; truly he succeeds who purifies it, and he fails who corrupts it." (Holy Quran 91:7-10)

HOW TO PLEASE AND WORSHIP GOD

Muslims believe that God sent the Holy Quran and the Holy Prophet Muhammad (peace be upon him) to teach us how to please and worship the One Creator:

"…There has come to you from God a light and a luminous Book (Holy Quran), through which God, by His grace, guides all who seek His good pleasure on the path of peace, and brings them out of the

depths of darkness into light and guides them unto a Straight Path."
(Holy Quran 5:15-16)

Good Deeds

Good, righteous deeds include giving charity, praying, keeping
promises, and being patient during hardships:

"It is not righteousness that you turn your faces east or west. But
it is righteousness to believe in God, and the Last Day, and the
Angels, and the Book, and the Messengers; to spend of your
substance, out of love for Him, for your kin, for orphans, for the
needy, for the wayfarer, for those who ask, and for the ransom of
slaves; to be steadfast in prayer, and practice regular charity, to fulfil
the contracts which ye have made; and to be firm and patient, in pain
(or suffering) and adversity, and throughout all periods of panic.
Such are the people of truth, the God-fearing."(Holy Quran 2:177)

Working for peace among people is a great deed that is better
than charity, fasting and prayer. The Prophet Muhammad (peace be
upon him) said:

"Do you know what is better than charity and fasting and prayer?
It is keeping peace and good relations between people, as quarrels
and bad feelings destroy mankind." (Recorded in Muslim & Bukhari)

Good deeds feel good, whereas bad deeds do not. The Prophet
Muhammad (peace be upon him) stated:

"Righteousness is in good character, and wrongdoing is that
which wavers in your soul and which you dislike people finding out
about." (recorded in Muslim)

Warnings to Humanity

The Quran and Hadiths warn humanity that they will be
accountable for their actions in this life:

"Say, 'It is God who gives you life, then makes you die; and in the end He shall gather you on the Day of Resurrection (the coming of) which is beyond all doubt, but most people do not understand. To God belongs the kingdom of the heavens and the earth. And on that Day when the Last Hour is come---on that Day all those who refused to believe (shall be) the real losers. And you shall see all people hobbling on their knees, for all people will be called upon to (face) their record: 'Today you shall be recompensed for all that you ever did. This is Our record, it speaks about you in all truth; for We had been recording all that you were doing.'" (Holy Quran 45:26-29)

"So he who does an atom's weight of good will see it, and he who does an atom's weight of evil will see it."(Holy Quran 99:7-8)

The Prophet Muhammad (peace be upon him) echoes this message of accountability:

"A man shall be asked concerning five (things) on the Day of Resurrection: concerning his life and how he spent it, concerning his youth and how he grew old, concerning his wealth: where he acquired it and in what way he spent it, and what was it that he did with the knowledge that he had." (Recorded in Tirmidhi)

"Three things follow a deceased: his family members, his wealth and his actions. Two of them return and one remains with him. His family members and wealth return, and his actions remain with him." (Recorded in Bukhari & Muslim)

EVEN OUR DIFFICULTIES HAVE A PURPOSE!

Our hardships in life have a purpose too: they are a test of our faith, and they also purify our souls:

"Do the people think that they will be left to say, "We believe," and they will not be tested?"

(Holy Quran 29:2)

The Prophet (peace be upon him) said:

"Whoever Allah wants good for him, he puts them to test. He puts them through difficulties, like a diamond or some metal that has to be burnt and then that which is bad from it is removed so that you have that which is the pure diamond or the pure gold..." (Recorded in Bukhari and Muslim)

In the end, we should remain patient and trust in God's promise:

"So patiently persevere: for verily the promise of Allah is true. Nor let those shake your firmness, who have (themselves) no certainty of faith." (Holy Quran 30:60)

TRUST IN GOD'S MERCY

In order to fulfil our purpose, we must trust in the kindness, goodness and mercy of Allah (swt):

"But those who do evil deeds then repent and believe, they will find your Lord Forgiving and Merciful." (The Holy Quran 7:153)

The Prophet Muhammad (peace be upon him) reported that the devil (satan) said to God: "I shall continue to lead Thy servants astray as long as their spirits are in their bodies." And God replied: "(Then) I shall continue to pardon them as long as they ask My forgiveness."(Recorded in Tirmidhi)

THE NEXT WORLD

Belief in a life purpose for the Muslim is closely tied to belief in the afterlife. Our worldly possessions will not last, but our good deeds done for God's sake will:

"Whatever you have will end, but whatever is with Allah is everlasting. And We will surely give those who were patient their reward according to the best of what they used to do." (Holy Quran 16:96)

"Know that the life of this world is play and a passing show, and adornment and boasting among you, and rivalry between you over piled up goods and children. It is like vegetation after a rain whose growth is pleasing to the farmers, but later it dries up and turns yellow and becomes straw stubble. And in the Final World there is a terrible chastisement and (also) forgiveness from God, and contentment. The present life is but the enjoyment of delusion." (Holy Quran 57:20)

"Every soul shall have a taste of death: And only on the Day of Judgment shall you be paid your full recompense. Only he who is saved far from the Fire and admitted to the Garden will have attained the object (of Life): For the life of this world is but goods and chattels of deception." (Holy Quran 3:185)

The next life is when we will see the fruits of our labours in this life:

The Prophet (peace be upon him) said that God the Exalted and Glorious has said: "I have prepared for My pious servants which no eye has ever seen, and no ear has ever heard, and no human heart has ever perceived, but it is testified by the Book of God." He then recited (the Quranic verse), "No soul knows what comfort has been concealed from it, as a reward for what it did." (Recorded in Muslim)

Lightning Source UK Ltd.
Milton Keynes UK
UKHW020646291021
393035UK00010B/554